**PLEASE
DO NOT TEAR OUT
RECIPES
PHOTOCOPY IF NECESSARY**

FARMERS' MARKETS OF THE HEARTLAND

P9-BZI-092

6/12

Heartland
Foodways

ublish
food
seed to
dwest.

Eisenhower Public Library
4613 N. Oketo Avenue
Harwood Heights, IL. 60706
708-867-7828

FARMERS' MARKETS
OF THE
HEARTLAND

Janine MacLachlan

UNIVERSITY OF ILLINOIS PRESS

Urbana, Chicago, and Springfield

Dedicated to the farmers, who feed our future.
And to my husband, Lauro Arias, who kept the home fires burning.

© 2012 by the Board of Trustees
of the University of Illinois

All rights reserved

Manufactured in the
United States of America
P 5 4 3 2 1

♾ This book is printed on acid-free paper.

Cataloging-in-Publication Data available from the Library of Congress
ISBN 978-0-252-07863-7 (paper : alk.)
ISBN 978-0-252-09419-4 (ebook)

University of Illinois Press
1325 South Oak Street
Champaign, IL 61820-6903
www.press.uillinois.edu

Designed by Erin Kirk New
Composed in 9.7/14 PMN Caecilia
Manufactured by Bang Printing

Contents

FARMERS' MARKETS OF THE HEARTLAND

Introduction

I cannot remember when I first started shopping at the farmers'
market, but I can tell you when my official food crush began. It
must have been late May in the early 1990s at a farmers' market in
Chicago. Thinking about dinner, with my mind *maybe* on carrots,
I was confronted with a table filled with about twenty varieties of
strawberries.

This dizzying array of vibrant red was enough to make me weak
at the knees. And they were friendly, too, labeled with enticing,
come-hither names like Earliglow, Rosa Linda, Jewel.

"Have a taste," said grower Lloyd Nichols. No hand slapping or
judgmental looks here at the open-air market. No feeling like I was
sneaking into the cookie jar before dinner. A row of quart containers stood at attention, all lined up like Rockettes at a Christmas
musical, separate from the sea of containers packed up for buying.
And Lloyd Nichols, farmer and father to three strapping sons, smil-
ing and saying, "Try a few."

Mind you, for the longest time my strawberries had come from the supermarket, all the way from California, hollow and white in the middle and tasting a little like cardboard mixed with water. But not Nichols's strawberries. Red all the way through, somehow heavy and with a bursting flavor like an actual living strawberry, the kind that grew in my friend's backyard that we would eat sitting between the rows, saving just a few to bring to the picnic table to dust with brown sugar and dip in whipped cream.

And when I compared Rhapsody to Pegasus, I realized they tasted different—delicious, but different. I suddenly understood what people mean when they talk about the impossibility of choosing between their children.

So this was the moment I fell in love with real strawberries, and with my farmers' market. And to this day I have yet to be convinced that any supermarket, even those rare ones that favor organic and local growers, come anywhere close to the open-air experience of discovering a new love.

This heady adventure was at the beginning of my personal local-food movement, years after Alice Waters began her own journey of working with farmers to supply ingredients for her legendary Berkeley restaurant, Chez Panisse. Years after, an act of Congress in 1976 laid the groundwork for the explosion of farmers' markets we see today.

But I was ahead of some people too. After years doing public relations in the food business, where I worked with Julia Child, Graham Kerr, Ina Garten, and a host of people we now call "celebrity chefs," I decided to check out the other side of the stove. I took classes at the Culinary Institute of America at Greystone, California, and then opened a cooking school, the Rustic Kitchen. Headquartered out of my home kitchen, I would invite a handful of people to come over and cook seasonal menus. I learned that not everyone shared my farmers' market food crush. "I don't have time to go to the farmers' market, Janine. I don't have time to add one more thing." This from an otherwise charming woman whose name I will protect for now.

My students taught me that although many people see the farmers' market as a place to buy food every week, to many it is an occasional curiosity, and to even more it is not on their radar screen. And when I learned that only 3 percent of food is sold at farmers' markets, I realized there is a lot of room to educate people about the value of buying local, the health benefits of fresh food, and the fun of shopping at farmers' markets.

If you are one of those people who are curious what the fuss is about with all this local food business, this book is for you.

Road Trip Research

I decided to explore the dynamics that feed a hungry audience, and I mapped out the middle of the country. With diligent research and a little throwing of a dart at a map, I embarked on a journey to learn about farmers' markets and food in the Midwest.

My process was carefully orchestrated and the most fun I have ever had. First, I scouted the best locations with tips from Slow Food friends, regional food and agriculture writers, even Facebook and Twitter. I scheduled market visits with the help of a spreadsheet that noted each market's days and hours, a dog-eared road atlas, and my trusty GPS system, nicknamed Sally.

And then I took to the road.

My road trips typically began on a Thursday, when I would stash a cooler in the trunk of my red Mustang and head to an afternoon market. The next day I would find a Friday market and sometimes visit a farm. I would get to bed early so as to arrive at my first Saturday market at the opening bell. After as many as four markets on a Saturday, I would then head back to Chicago to sift through my notes and photos, schedule follow-up interviews, and conduct additional research with organizations that advocate for small farms and local food.

I met people saving livestock breeds recently slated for extinction, along with farmers growing heirloom fruit and new varieties of vegetables. I found artisans making cheese and bread and jam. One farmers' market had a festival-like atmosphere, with live entertainment, locally roasted coffee and artisan pastry, chef demonstrations every hour, all in the friendly confines of a leafy park. Moms with strollers mingle with chefs in white jackets or in unshaven incognito. Other markets were more utilitarian, on asphalt with easy parking. Today, if you are interested in food, you are at the farmers' market.

The first thing I learned in researching this book is that people are passionate about their farmers' markets, that just about everyone believes that their producers are the most talented, taste-focused growers. People love their farmers almost the way they love their children and the way my father loves the Michigan State Spartans.

I met elk ranchers, heirloom orchard owners, young twentysomethings in their first season of farming, and growers on their great-great-grandfather's farm at the market with their grandchildren, telling me about six generations devoted to the land. I met fellow farm groupies who shared my emotional attachment to their growers. Again and again, I was warned that I would be missing out if I did not see this market or visit that farm. And I was warmed by the passion, devotion, and dedication that all these people felt. I would introduce myself to one producer, and within minutes people were tapping my shoulder to tell me about a course on food policy or a farm stand on the way to the interstate.

In Minnesota I learned about rural food deserts, in Milwaukee about small-scale urban agriculture. I ate cherries in Michigan, popcorn in Indiana, and pie everywhere. I felt uplifted every time I got back into the car, but always wistful about that person I did not meet.

My goal here is to present this book as a kind of album, a collection of stories that together represent a snapshot of farmers' markets. I hope you will embark on your own adventure and gather your own collection of growers.

The Backstory

Farmers' markets are a powerful force, given that less than 3 percent of our nation's food is sold there. It is worth taking a look at how we got to this place where the market is the new town square, the place where chefs solidify reputations, where food politics are debated.

Selling direct to consumers used to be the norm, even before the influx of Europeans transformed this continent to an agrarian nation, when it was populated with Indian tribes who traded extensively with each other. In *The Farmers' Market Book: Growing Food, Cultivating Community,* authors and farmers Jennifer Meta Robinson and J. A. Hartenfeld tell about a native American Indian market near what is modern-day St. Louis. The settlement was at its height between the years 1000 and 1150 and had ten thousand to twenty thousand residents. Archeological records of the site indicate evidence of extensive trade.

As our country was being settled by Europeans, trading posts were the place people—particularly fur traders—obtained goods. And when we moved to a more settled era, markets became an important part of life not only to obtain goods, but also to exchange news. Later, cities built large sheds to house farmers as a center for trade, and many of these markets still exist as broker markets, including the Eastern Market in Detroit, West Side Market in Cleveland, Findlay Market in Cincinnati, and Soulard in St. Louis. A broker market is one where food is imported from far-flung areas and later sold to consumers, restaurants, and retailers.

In the 1940s farmers' markets all but disappeared as small farms declined and grocery store chains consolidated their purchasing. The advances in transportation that brought fresh milk to cities three times a day continued to progress. It used to be that individual grocers had relationships with their own stable of farmers, but as grocery store chains expanded, they consolidated and required their supplier farms to be bigger and bigger to match their growing store count. Today, food travels an average of fifteen hundred miles to reach the supermarket.

One of the big players in this trend was grocery store chain A&P, or Great Atlantic and Pacific Tea Company. Even the name reflects the lofty goals of a supermarket chain to make one-stop shopping available for the busy homemaker. But something happened in our quest for convenience: we sacrificed taste. Flavor became an afterthought in our pursuit of food prized for shelf life and ease of shipping.

Of course, other factors fed the decline of the farmers' market. After World War II, chemical companies turned their attention toward using new technology, giving us chemical fertilizers and pesticides that bumped up yields. Only later would we learn about environmental degradation. Other techniques developed to feed the troops on the battlefield were translated into convenience foods that reduced mom's need to cook.

The decline of open-air markets continued as ideas of sanitation changed. Outdoor markets were considered dirty because confined indoor spaces were easier to clean. But in 1976, Congress passed the Farm-to-Consumer Direct Marketing Act, paving the way for farmers to connect with their buyers. The United States Department of Agriculture Census has documented the growth since then. It has really been in the past fifteen years or so that farmers' markets have taken off. In 1994 there were 1,775 in the United States; in 2010 that number swelled to 6,132.

Today's Markets and Trends

In recent years there has been more talk about why markets are more popular than ever. Local food advocates assert that food grown for shipping cannot possibly be more flavorful than food grown for taste. Megafacilities have become hotbeds of foodborne illness. The first decade of our new century saw illnesses caused by tainted spinach, peanuts, meat, and eggs. Employees at processing plants have videotaped other employees abusing animals. Thus, it makes sense that one of the reasons many people flock to farmers' markets is that they know where their food has been. Buyers trust the people who sell there, because they have a relationship with the producer.

Farmers receive less than 10 percent of every dollar spent at the grocery store. At the farmers' market, the grower receives 100 percent.

Beyond food safety, many eaters realize that two factors, taste and connection, fuel their desire to shop a farmers' market. It is not because it is easier—people still need to visit a supermarket for Tide and toothpaste, items every household needs but cannot buy at any farmers' market. It takes a special trip to buy the local produce, artisan breads, and pasture-raised meat that one finds at the farmers' market. Because it involves a special trip, a plan, and a pile of canvas bags, shoppers must perceive a value, and it is not convenience. Production issues aside, savvy cooks today know that no amount of technique can save a tired carrot, a watery tomato, or a rock-hard peach.

In the face of industrialization, even the USDA recognizes the importance of supporting the small producer. The organization's 2011 budget included $10 million in grants to promote farmers' markets, up from zero only five years before. We will talk more about the USDA's Farmers Market Promotion Program in the Missouri chapter.

Bruce Sherman is chef-partner at North Pond in Chicago and chair of Chefs Collaborative, a national network of chefs who advocate for sustainably produced food and facilitate farmer/chef relationships. The group is at the forefront of sustainability issues in foodservice and hosts an annual summit to share ideas and information about promoting a more sustainable food system.

Bruce Sherman, chef/partner at North Pond, with his wife, Joan

Sherman is the real deal, often buying food at the farmers' market during the day and serving it for dinner a few hours later. He takes advantage of every flavor of the season, including the first radishes, and demonstrates his recipe for radish butter as an easy, flavorful way to enjoy this tasty root.

Radish Butter

Bruce Sherman, North Pond

Radishes are fast-growing, deliciously bitter roots, coveted for their spicy, pungent flavor. Their seeds also hold up against early spring chill and are therefore one of the first vegetables to appear at farmers' markets. The radish is a classic partner to rich butter, and Sherman has created the perfect blend to serve in a crock with toast points.

MAKES ABOUT 1 CUP

3 large radishes, sliced julienne style

8 tablespoons butter (1 stick), room temperature

Juice of ¼ lemon (about 1 tablespoon)

2 tablespoons fresh mint leaves, chopped

1 tablespoon minced fresh chives

1 tablespoon chopped, fresh, flat-leaf parsley

Salt and pepper to taste

Using an electric mixer, beat the butter until smooth. Add lemon juice and beat until smooth, then add chopped herbs. Turn off the mixer and gently fold in the radishes. Season with salt and pepper.

Why Shop at the Farmers' Market?

The primary reason to shop at a farmers' market, of course, is flavor. It is the easiest way to get the freshest, most flavorful food, which is why you will find a lot of chefs there. The most *important* reason is the relationships you will create with your growers and your community. The farmers' market is the new town square, where people gather.

Of course, there are other essential reasons. Shopping there is the easiest way to participate in a food system that promotes animal welfare and environmentally responsible growing practices, for the simple reason that you can talk to the producer and ask how they grow things. And many market managers will visit the farms to scout things out firsthand. All in all, shopping a farmers' market is the best way to stay close to your food and find delicious discoveries for your supper table.

How to Shop the Farmers' Market

Go early. Producers will have more time to talk, and you will be able to linger at the table without a crowd pressing in behind you. Fill your canvas bag, then relax with a crusty loaf and enjoy some people watching.

Research the market's policies. A producer-only market requires the farmer to be behind the table. Some emphasize organic growers. Understand how the market polices itself and decide what is important to you.

Embrace seasonality. Come with a plan, but be flexible. Know how many meals you will want to cook in the coming days, how much fruit for snacking, etc. But do not insist on specific ingredients. An abundance of onions might inspire you to make a savory tart one week; the next week, the first broccoli rabe means a pasta dinner. Strive to try a new food every week.

Strike up a conversation. Ask the producer about growing practices. Some growers are also avid cooks, and fellow shoppers will have plenty of tips about ingredient combinations. They will tell you the gnarly knob is celeriac and is great with mayo.

Bring a cooler. If you want fragile greens or perishable dairy products, it is a good idea to have a cooler in case you are delayed on your way home, or you want to stick around for lunch.

Shadow a chef. In a lot of urban areas the chefs will shop at markets, particularly those on Wednesday, where they can stock up for the busy weekend. Ask them whom they like to buy from.

Come home and prep. Sauté your kale with garlic once you get home and store it in fridge containers. Caramelize a batch of onions. Also learn what foods might be fragile and should be washed right before cooking. Rinse berries only just before cooking or eating, for instance, because they have a natural barrier that protects them from deterioration.

Look for canning classes. "Putting up" food is back in vogue as people discover the distinctive flavor from making home-made marinara or apricot Riesling jam to enjoy in the dark winter months.

Consider a CSA membership. Community Supported Agriculture (CSA) is discussed more in the Illinois chapter because it is the locale of the world's largest CSA, operated by the colorful Farmer John. Essentially, CSA is a farm subscription wherein you pay at the beginning of the season and pick your share of the bounty each week, and you will receive volume discounts.

Chicago

Because my romance with farmers began here, and because it was home base for my research road trip, we will begin in Chicago, the largest city in the Midwest. At first glance, Chicago's urban canyons may not seem the most likely place to explore agriculture. But this metropolis is a center for food advocates dedicated to bringing fresh, nourishing food to its citizens. In fact, the dynamic local food culture in this city is in stark contrast to that of the vast rural regions, those remote areas of many heartland states where there are fewer small, diversified farms and thus fewer farmers' markets. People who do not maintain their own vegetable gardens are obliged to shop at the nearest supermarket, in many cases miles away, and those supermarkets stock produce from even farther locales. This disparity in food cultures throughout the region illustrates only one of the many challenges of access to fresh, local food.

Thus, urban centers like Chicago, with hungry eaters looking for fresh seasonal food who have the pocketbooks to afford it, make an ideal market for, well, markets. The city of Chicago farmers' market program began in 1979 and now has more than twenty distinct farmers' markets in the downtown core and in neighborhoods scattered across the metro area.

Best Gig Ever: Farm Forager

In 2006 Chicago hired its first "farm forager" to visit farms and recruit them to participate in the city's farmers' markets. Why would a city with abundant clientele need to recruit farmers? Because farmers, like many people, often decide to skip the traffic congestion and parking challenges and settle in the suburbs. Intrepid farmers who make the trek to the city say that the volume of customers keeps them coming back.

Farm forager Dave Rand

Dave Rand's job as farm forager for the city of Chicago and the Green City Market calls for him to travel five states recruiting growers to join the city's extensive farmers' market network. His role is to enlist farmers into the network, to scout production practices to ensure high standards, and also to police vendors, who sometimes "stretch" the idea of local and seasonal food.

"Monitoring the markets to ensure that only local foods are on the table is an interesting challenge these days," Rand says. "The seasonality chart has changed in recent years, in part because of climate change, but also because growers are using hoop houses and other methods to extend the growing season." In other words, it is harder to spot at market the renegade food from outside a local area when our growing season is lengthening. So Rand visits dozens of growers each season to see firsthand what is in their soil.

Such diligence in market monitoring was not always the norm. A decade ago, vendors would go to Chicago's famed Fulton wholesale district, pick up nonlocal tomatoes months before they were in season in Illinois, and then sell them at area farmers markets without notifying patrons that they were reselling wholesale produce. Today the entire system has evolved so that vendors are now required to adhere to strict guidelines about what constitutes locally grown and to clearly label foods that are not grown on their acreage.

And still, cheaters abound. A 2010 case in Los Angeles made national news and sent the Internet aflutter when a farmers' market worker said she felt threatened because she reported another vendor for allegedly repackaging produce from Mexico. Small-scale, locally produced food often comes at a premium price and, just as with other businesses, unscrupulous people are willing to take advantage. Although rare, these incidents illustrate the importance of having a relationship with your growers and spending time getting to know them.

Chicago markets are operated through the Mayor's Office of Special Events, and Rand's salary is split between the city and a private not-for-profit market, Chicago's Green City Market. Rand explains that this market outside the city system is said to have started in part as a reaction against the loose supervision over city markets at the time.

Rand serves on the board of the Farmers Market Coalition, a national resource for market organizers, who can access its resource library for information on how to create a successful farmers' market.

Chicago's Green City Market

Founded 1998

55+ vendors

Wednesdays and
Saturdays, May
through November

South end of Lincoln
Park between Clark
Street and Stockton
Drive, Chicago

Indoors during the
off season

Stroll through the Green City Market and you see just about anything you might like to eat: beef, chicken, elk, eggs, vegetables and fruits, honey, maple syrup, and also prepared foods like pasta, tomato and mushroom sauces, pies, scones, and cookies.

For hungry folks who cannot wait to get home with their purchases, there is Abby's Crepe Stand, named after the market's late founder Abby Mandel; fruit smoothies at Seedling Fruit; even grilled burgers by Sunday Dinner using beef from Heartland Meats. It is a lively, vibrant place in leafy Lincoln Park, Chicago's largest public park, designed by renowned landscape architect Jens Jensen. The experience includes chef demonstrations, live music, and a children's education program called Club Sprouts, operated by Purple Asparagus, where children can taste and smell the food and learn about who grew it for them.

Green City did not begin as the pretty, popular market it is today. It started with a half-dozen vendors in an alley behind the Chicago Theater on State Street in the Loop, where vendors were in competition with dumpsters, and shoppers needed to sidestep potholes filled with whatever shimmering liquid had leaked from the trash. Green City now operates all year, outdoors in Lincoln Park May through October, and lately at the Peggy Notebaert Nature Museum during the chillier months. With fifty-five vendors at last count, it is considered the premier market in the city, drawing vendors from Illinois, Michigan, Indiana, and Wisconsin.

It is worth a moment to meet the doyenne of local organic eating, Alice Waters. Her Berkeley, California, restaurant, Chez Panisse, is mecca for many locavores who make a pilgrimage to eat the style of cuisine she inspired based on ingredients just moments out of the earth. She went on to establish the Edible Schoolyard, a program that started a school garden in Berkeley and used it for teaching science, and also served the food in the school cafeteria. It has served as a model for school gardens across the country.

The influence of Alice Waters cannot be overstated, and Green City organizers were thrilled when she named Green City one of the top ten markets in the United States. Another of her favorites is the Dane County Market in Madison, which we will visit in the Wisconsin chapter.

Under the guidance of market founder Abby Mandel and a steering committee of chefs and food-loving volunteers, Green City is often called out as a leader in local food systems. What separates Green City from other Chicago-area markets, say organizers, is the higher level of scrutiny of the producers. Abby Mandel passed away in 2008, but her legacy remains with a strong board, substantial fundraising, and devoted volunteers.

Why the tireless effort to keep Green City Market strong? Because local food should be universal, says Sarah Stegner, celebrated chef/partner of Prairie Grass Café and Prairie Fire, who was there at the start. Stegner joined forces with Abby Mandel because she believed that local, farm-produced food should be for everyone, not just her high-end restaurant patrons at the Ritz-Carlton, where she was cooking at the time. "Another reason, honestly, is to help secure this food for the restaurants too," she adds. "We need to be sure these farmers can stay in business so we can continue to buy from them."

Like many markets across the Midwest, Green City conducts major fundraising to keep everything going. One popular public event is the annual barbecue launched by Les Dames d'Escoffier, a professional group of women leaders in the food profession. Each July a sold-out crowd of about five hundred mingles with growers and chefs who prepare dishes based on market ingredients.

And the chefs rally to the event, as they do to the weekly chef demos at the market. Recipes at the demos are deliciously simple and designed to showcase peak-of-season ingredients, like rhubarb ice cream from television's Top Chef winner Stephanie Izard, radish butter from Bruce Sherman of North Pond, sour cherry basil jam from Paul Virant of Vie in Westerns Springs, and red cabbage with apples and bacon from Dana Benigno of ChicagoCooks.com and Sweet Girl Desserts. Not limited to fruits and vegetables, Brian Huston of The Publican—known for his devotion to pork—demonstrated a recipe for his signature potted *rillettes*. But organizers are constantly vigilant, and they turned away a chef who intended to demonstrate citrus dishes. Of course: citrus does not grow in the midwestern climate.

Farmers at Chicago's Green City Market

As with most farmers' markets, Green City purveyors are a mix of career changers, entrepreneurs, and people who are farming acreage handed down from their grandparents. People who work the tables shoulder to shoulder with the producers are often culinary students, food writers, and sustainability advocates. Each grower has a story, and here are just a few from producers based in Illinois.

Dave and Sue Cleverdon,
Kinnickinnick Farm

》 Dave Cleverdon farms at **Kinnikinnick Farm** in Caledonia, eighty miles northwest of Chicago in Boone County. Cleverdon and wife Susan set up shop at Kinnikinnick in 1992 on acreage that was first under cultivation in 1849 and had stayed in the same family for generations. Cleverdon set out to differentiate his offerings by emphasizing Italian greens—even going so far as to buy seeds from Italian seed companies, a novel practice at the time. Now his Bietina, Cavolo Nero, and Minestra Nera varieties show up at the Green City and Evanston markets, and also on the tables at restaurants like Blackbird and North Pond in Chicago. Kinnikinnick is the only midwestern farm to participate in Feather Down Farm Days, a program where visitors can stay overnight in well-appointed tents on the property. Cleverdon also serves as a board member for Green City and the Frontera Farmer Foundation, and he consistently reminds people that the average age of farmers is approaching sixty, and thus we need more young farmers.

» Lloyd Nichols—whom I first met as I was experiencing berry nirvana—has farmed in Marengo on **Nichols Farm and Orchard** since 1978, along with wife Doreen and sons Chad, Nick, and Todd. Together with their staff they sell at fifteen markets throughout the Chicago metropolitan area. Nichols was one of the original six vendors at the market in 1998, which marked his twentieth anniversary as a farmer. He began small, as more of a hobby farmer after a career in the Navy; today the operation is 250 acres. Their specialty is variety, and a visit to their booth can be a head-spinning experience as you choose from twenty varieties of strawberries in late spring, or the dozens of potato and apple varieties in autumn.

» Green City is also home to three vendors that double as job-training initiatives. **Growing Home** teaches skills to homeless and low-income people. **Growing Power** is a national nonprofit based in Milwaukee. We will meet Growing Power founder Will Allen in the Wisconsin chapter. And the **Chicago Honey Co-op** has produced honey and trained difficult-to-employ people since 2004.

Michael Thompson is the force behind Chicago Honey Co-op, a one-hundred-hive apiary with twenty million bees on an otherwise blighted corner of Chicago's west side. The bees enjoy a veritable buffet as they pollinate the city's treasure trove of flowers in diminutive back yards and expansive parks, including Millennium Park in the heart of downtown. And because seasonal flowers are always in bloom, the honey changes flavor as the seasons evolve, beginning with a pale color from sweet clover, with a light, almost vanilla flavor, to a deep spicy amber from later blooms. All this bounty yields about two hundred pounds of honey per hive each year.

Thompson holds another distinctive title: he is chief beekeeper to the mayor. Longtime mayor Richard Daley, who made no secret of his vision to make Chicago greener, initiated a green-roof program, beginning with City Hall. Thompson manages the apiary kept on the roof to pollinate plants on the 30,000-square-foot rooftop garden several stories up. Thompson teaches a beekeeping class every January and has seen interest in beekeeping skyrocket.

In addition to rich, flavorful honey, the co-op offers another benefit: it trains hard-to-employ individuals in beekeeping and business skills—perhaps the sweetest result of this beekeeping enterprise and the most important byproduct of the honey.

An anecdote from one sunny Wednesday illustrates the impact of this successful job-training initiative. A chef demonstrator was setting up at Green City, and a big burly (frankly tough-looking) guy with tattooed knuckles came over and started organizing the station, setting up tables, hooking up the electricity.

"Are you a staffer at the market?" said the chef.

"No, I'm a beekeeper." It was said with such pride that one can only guess about how it must feel to be surrounded by people who admire what you do.

» Tracey Vowell is co-owner with Kathe Roybal, her partner in farming and life, of the nine-acre **Three Sisters Garden** in Kankakee. Before becoming a farmer herself, Vowell was managing chef at Frontera Grill for a number of years, where she developed relationships with growers who work with that famed restaurant. Her farm is named after the Native American practice of growing corn, beans, and squash in the same mounds of earth. According to that tradition, corn is planted in the center of a plot, and the corn stalk serves as a stake for the beans to climb. Squash surrounds the perimeter. The idea represents the symbiotic nature of traditional growing. From a practical standpoint, the Indians had learned how intensive planting can help grow more food on a smaller plot. The offerings at the Three Sisters market table are decidedly different from other growers, including organic dried black beans and rolled oats grown on additional acreage near their original farm.

One of the most treasured offerings from Three Sisters Garden is not grown on their farm but rather on a family operation farther afield. Because of the unusual nature of the food, Three Sisters successfully obtained permission to sell it in Chicago. Vowell and her parents harvest pecans from trees on the family's three-hundred-acre forest in northwest Tennessee. The Vowells have served as stewards of this land for more than one hundred years by harvesting hardwood for fine furniture veneers, choosing individual trees to be harvested rather than clear cutting sections the way timber companies might. Interspersed in the woods are pecan trees, which can take up to forty years to reach full fruit.

Foraging wild nuts is not an easy task. First the Vowells spread tarps downhill and anchor them, then return to collect the fallen nuts. The good news is that pecans are tidier than other tree nuts, splitting into four pieces and dropping to the ground. Cracking businesses used to abound in the area, and there are still a few left. A machine feeds nuts one by one to be cracked, then Vowell and Roybal pick out the pecan meat by hand. The flavor is beyond fresh. Vowell obtained a special dispensation to sell the nuts at the market.

Allowing the sale of these pecans represents a rare departure for Green City and was not without controversy. Vowell was able to make the case that the artisan nature of the harvesting and family stewardship of the land makes it worthy. But others contest that Tennessee woods origin, more than four hundred miles from Chicago, are too far to be considered local.

» Paula Haney's business card states that she's the "proud owner" of the **Hoosier Mama Pie Company**. She used the Green City Market as an incubator for her pie company before opening her shop, and still sells here. Haney hails from Indiana (as her company name implies) and was pastry chef who worked with celebrity chefs Shawn McClain and Grant Achatz at Trio in Evanston. After careful research into vintage baking, Haney created her own all-butter crust and started experimenting with flavor combinations based on area fruit. She says her vinegar chess pie is also called "desperation pie." The original idea was created before grocery stores provided out-of-season food and people were desperate for something sweet. For Haney, it is what she sells at Green City's winter market since organizers adhere to strict criteria about local ingredients—you won't spot banana cream or chocolate pies at the market since those ingredients require a tropical climate. We will talk more with Haney in the chapter about her native state of Indiana.

Vinegar Chess Pie

Paula Haney, Hoosier Mama Pie Company, Chicago

Although the lineage of the name "chess pie" remains a mystery, some say that the name is a variation of the phrase "just pie." The secret to the tender texture of Haney's crust is the combination of chilled and frozen butter, yet there is something to her technique as well. She has a flow chart illustrating how to achieve the perfect consistency.

MAKES ONE 10-INCH PIE

1¼ cup granulated sugar

7 tablespoons unsalted butter, room temperature

3 eggs

1 tablespoon cornmeal

1½ tablespoons apple cider vinegar

1 teaspoon pure vanilla extract

1 10-inch unbaked pie shell (recipe follows)

Preheat oven to 300 degrees and position rack in the center. Using an electric mixer on medium speed, cream the butter and sugar until light. Add eggs one at a time and mix until blended. Add cornmeal, then vinegar and vanilla. Pour into unbaked pie shell. Bake for 20 minutes, then rotate pie 180 degrees. Continue baking until golden and cracked, another 20 to 25 minutes.

Vinegar chess pie at Hoosier Mama Pie Company

Hoosier Mama Pie Pastry

MAKES ONE DOUBLE-CRUST PIE OR TWO SINGLE-CRUST PIES

2¼ cups all-purpose flour, frozen

1 teaspoon salt

1 teaspoon sugar

9 tablespoons unsalted butter, chilled, cut into ¾-inch cubes

5 tablespoons unsalted butter, frozen, cut into ¾-inch cubes

1 tablespoon cider or red wine vinegar

7 tablespoons ice water

Pour flour, salt, and sugar into a food processor fitted with a metal blade. Pulse to combine. In a small bowl, stir together vinegar and ice water. Add chilled butter to flour and pulse about 20 seconds until it resembles coarse meal. Add frozen butter and pulse again until butter is the size of peas. Add five tablespoons vinegar water and pulse six times. Remove cover and pinch the dough. If it is still in particles but holds together when pinched between your fingers, it is ready. If it falls apart, add another tablespoon of vinegar water and pulse three times. Do the pinch test again. If the dough still does not hold together when pinched, add one more tablespoon of vinegar water and pulse three times. Turn the dough onto a floured board and divide in two. Knead each into a ball until the dough holds together and is slightly stretchy. Wrap in plastic and refrigerate for at least an hour or overnight.

When ready to roll out the crust, remove from refrigerator and let rest for ten minutes or so. Roll the pastry on a floured surface using a floured pin to make a 13-inch round, rolling from the center to the edge of the dough in all directions. To keep the dough from sticking, periodically loosen and rotate it.

Transfer the dough into the tart pan by folding it in half over the rolling pin and sliding it over to the pan. Trim and crimp the edges.

>> Like Paula Haney at Hoosier Mama Pie Company, Nancy Silver of **Snookelfritz** started in the pastry chef world and now sells ice cream by the pint at Green City. As pastry chef at the former Mod and a number of other restaurants, Silver experimented with making ice cream until she refined her perfect formula. Her flavors range from roasted strawberry mascarpone in late spring to salted caramel apple in the fall, and honey crème fraiche throughout the year. She uses ingredients from fellow market vendors, including milk from **Kilgus Dairy**, a seventy-five-cow dairy in Fairbury, Illinois. Flora Lazar makes exceptional *pâté de fruits* under the banner **Flora's Confections**.

>> **Becker Lane Organic Pork** is a nationally known vendor raising USDA-certified Berkshire and Cheshire White pigs. Jude Becker shuns the confinement practices found on large commercial pork farms and builds moveable "huts" for his pigs to live; then he can move the dwellings to reveal fertilized soil perfect for growing crops to feed the pigs in the winter, when they are not on pasture. His latest offering is prosciutto made from acorn-fed pigs.

>> Other vendors include **Dietzler Farms**, **Hawk's Hill Elk Ranch**, **Ellis Farm**, **Iron Creek Farms**, and **Mick Klug Farms**, to name just a few. We will meet **Green Acres Farm**, **Capriole**, and **Burton's Maplewood Farm** in the Indiana chapter; **Seedling Fruit** in the Michigan chapter; and **Prairie Fruits Farm** in the Illinois chapter.

And Green City has offerings that guarantee no one has to shop on an empty stomach. Bakeries **Floriole** and **Bennison's** serve up scones, rolls, and brioche for nibbling with **Intelligentsia Coffee**, and the market crepe stand offers fillings of sweet fruits and savory vegetables and cheese. Chef-owners Christine Cikowsky and Josh Kulp of **Sunday Dinner/Eat Green Foods** grill burgers with **Heartland Meats Piemontese Beef**.

Mick Klug's farm has been in his family for more than eighty years, and he has been a strong presence at Chicago markets for more than thirty

Poached Farm Egg over Crisp Polenta and Summer Vegetable Relish

Sarah Stegner, Prairie Fire and Prairie Grass Café

Market founder and chef Sarah Stegner (Prairie Fire and Prairie Grass Café) and partner-chef George Bumbaris have a longstanding record of working with local producers. One of Stegner's favorite products is Tracey Vowell's ground-to-order polenta. When Stegner gets polenta to use in her kitchen, it has often been milled less than twenty-four hours before.

What is so special about fresh-ground polenta? Vowell explains that grains, being seeds, are "perfect little storage packages." When the "package" is broken, deterioration begins, and thus the starch quality and vibrant corn flavor begins to diminish soon after milling.

"We got a white corn hybrid seed from a neighbor farmer," Vowell says, and now they save the seed and plant it from year to year. At harvest time, they use a combine to remove the husks and shell the kernels off the cob. Then they double clean the corn, first using a barrel cleaner that sifts the seed through a screen, then sending the grain through a fanning mill to remove any remaining bits of stalk and cob. In 2010 Three Sisters produced almost four hundred bushels, and they intend to double that production to accommodate demand. "We never dreamed it would be so popular," Vowell says.

SERVES FOUR, WITH SOME LEFTOVER POLENTA

Polenta

¼ cup polenta

1¼ cup whole milk

Pinch salt

1 tablespoon unsalted butter

1 tablespoon grated Brunkow aged cheddar (or your favorite strong local cheese)

Put milk in medium saucepan over medium heat. As it begins to steam, add the polenta stirring frequently. Cook, stirring occasionally, until very thick. Stir in butter and cheese. Pour into a buttered 8" x 8" pan. Cool completely. If making the polenta ahead, store covered with plastic wrap in the refrigerator. Using a two-inch round cookie cutter or glass, cut eight rounds from the polenta. You will have enough polenta to make more if you like, or save the remaining polenta for another use.

Poached Eggs

1 tablespoon white vinegar

8 farm eggs

Add vinegar to about three inches of water in a large skillet. Bring to a simmer over medium heat. Crack each egg into a large spoon and gently slide into the water—you may need to work in batches depending on the size of your pan. Cook until the whites are firm and the yolks still runny, about 4-5 minutes. If you're new at poaching, you may want to include an extra "test egg" to determine your desired doneness. Remove with a slotted spoon and drain on a towel.

Summer Vegetable Relish

2 tablespoons olive oil

2 tablespoons chopped green onion

½ cup chopped fresh tomato

½ cup fresh corn kernels

2 tablespoon chopped chives, basil, and parsley

¼ cup shaved Brunkow aged cheddar (or whatever cheese you used in the polenta)

Preheat a small skillet over medium heat. Add the olive oil and green onions, and sauté until lightly crisp. Add the fresh tomatoes and sauté for 3 to 4 minutes until they begin to soften. Add the corn and cook another minute. Transfer to mixing bowl and stir in the herbs and cheese.

   Assembly: reheat the same skillet over high heat. Add two tablespoons olive oil and sauté polenta on both sides until crispy. Put two polenta circles on a plate. Put a hot poached egg on top of each circle. Spoon the relish over the eggs.

Frontera Farmer Foundation:
A Culinary Microclimate

Rick Bayless is the guiding force behind his organization's focus on quality ingredients. He has a long list of envy-inspiring titles: chef, restaurateur, author, TV host, and winner of Top Chef Master, a season of Bravo TV's popular program focused on accomplished chefs rather than up-and-comers. He is widely considered America's expert on Mexican cuisine. Yet he has come to this place of culinary superstardom not by opening restaurants in every city. For years he operated only two: Frontera Grill and Topolobampo, side by side and, in late 2009, he added Xoco, a casual spot in an adjoining space. But one can argue that his most important accomplishment is away from the limelight.

Bayless believes that restaurants are crucial to the success of growers who sell at farmers' markets. "The amount of tomatoes a restaurant will use in a week far surpasses the amount a family eats," he told me on a farm field trip organized by some Wisconsin growers. That quantity can make all the difference in the success of a farm's fiscal year. Bayless's restaurants have a longstanding reputation of working with local growers.

He tells about a staff meeting in 2003 when someone was vetting yet another request for the restaurant to participate in a fundraiser. Restaurant people are notoriously generous, and the idea of feeding people for a good cause is difficult to resist. Still, managing chef Tracey Vowell said, "Wouldn't it be great to focus more efforts on causes closer to Frontera's heart?"—namely, the growers.

And from that offhand comment at a staff meeting came the beginning of the Frontera Farmer Foundation, which in its first five years gave more than $500,000 to small farms that supply the restaurants. Projects include expanding herds of pasture-raised cattle, installing irrigation systems, and building hoop houses, barns, and portable chicken coops. These projects may often make the difference between profit and loss for a small farmer—or, for that matter, just staying in business. An independent committee reviews applications. Perhaps it is this devotion to taste that starts way before any ingredients get to the kitchen that makes Frontera a more interesting place to cook. It is not about moving meals through. There is a spirit of engagement.

Frontera Grill managing chef Brian Enyart is the one who referred to Frontera Foods as a microclimate. A microclimate, by definition, is a local atmospheric zone where the climate differs from the surrounding area. In this case Frontera differs from a lot of restaurants, probably most restaurants, because its employees stay considerably longer than staff at other places. Often restaurant cooks believe they can advance faster if they jump around every few years, or even every few months. Enyart has been with Frontera since 1996, and he is not the only employee with such tenure.

As managing chef, Enyart spends an inordinate amount of time sourcing ingredients. He can do this, he says, because Frontera has superior staff retention in a business not known for longevity. He explains, "We don't burn through a lot of cooks so we can focus on the food instead of showing people how to find the washroom."

Grower relationships are important here. Enyart talks about meeting Marty Travis of Spence Farm, a family operation in Fairbury, Illinois, about one hundred miles southwest of Chicago in Livingston County. Travis showed up at the back door with a crate of ramps, wild onions of early spring. Later Travis introduced him to the paw paw, a native midwestern tree fruit that is delicious to eat but a challenge to harvest.

If you have never seen a paw paw, they are the color of a green pear, with soft, creamy flesh the color of banana and flavor that is almost tropical, like a papaya crossed with mango. It has a row of black seeds the size of black beans running through the center. Because it is difficult to harvest—and to eat for that matter—it fell out of favor to the point where it is now considered endangered. It is found primarily on older trees that farmers have kept around for their own use.

With regard to another specialty ingredient, Enyart told Travis about his mission to serve Iroquois white cornmeal at Frontera. He had been buying the cornmeal from the Iroquois nation in New York state, but the chief had passed away and new tribal leaders had decided not to grow it anymore. Travis was intrigued and started tracking down seed suppliers. He found two, but one had already discontinued the seed. The supplier charged $50 a pound for the seed—a breathtaking amount, given that typical seed corn goes for $7 to $10 a pound. Travis ordered 1.5 pounds, enough for eight rows two hundred feet long.

"It was horrible looking," Travis says. "Terribly buggy, and it fell over in a wind storm." The "bugginess" came predominantly from the rootworm beetle. Since Travis's farm is surrounded by fields of commodity corn produced with chemical inputs, both good and bad bugs evacuate for more welcoming pastures. That first harvest, Travis netted sixty-three pounds of cornmeal and nine pounds of seed. Chef Enyart bought it all and requested eight hundred pounds of cornmeal for the following year, more than ten times the initial harvest. This would require fifteen pounds of seed. "I was six pounds short," Travis says.

By then the supplier was selling the seed *by the kernel,* 250 kernels for $20. And they only had five pounds. Travis negotiated the same $50-per-pound price from the previous year and bought the entire lot. That growing season he harvested twelve hundred pounds of cornmeal and sold eight hundred to Frontera, giving him four hundred pounds to sell to other restaurants and to eager cooks who gladly spent more on shipping than on the $15 for a pound of cornmeal. Some of the eighty pounds of seed went to other farms in Iowa and Nebraska.

But seed is only the first expense. The corn is harvested by hand, and anything hand-picked is more expensive by virtue of the labor costs. The corn is then roasted in the husk over an oak fire, then husked and milled on site. The taste? Phenomenal, say chefs, in part because of the distinctive flavor from the roasting process.

The year-three harvest yielded 5,000 pounds of corn. And now Travis is credited with saving a food that might have become extinct. The Frontera Farmer Foundation supported Spence Farm by underwriting a custom grill for roasting the Iroquois white corn, and later for a stone mill to keep the grinding process closer to home.

"Conventional agriculture is not that interesting," Travis says. "I'd rather find a niche, then develop it." The next niche for Spence Farm is the Kickapoo bean, named because a member of the Kickapoo Indian tribe gave the beans to Travis's fourth great grandfather to help sustain the family after an 1830 blizzard. The beans became a family legend, and somehow Travis tracked down a handful from a distant relative. Right now Travis is growing only for seed, but the first crop will be ready in a few years.

Farm Stand at City Farm: Social Justice and Urban Agriculture

Tuesday through
Saturday afternoons,
July through September

Clybourn Avenue and
Division Street

Sometimes a farm has such a great location that shoppers can shop right at the farm just as conveniently as at the market. It is rare to find a farm so close to downtown, but City Farm enjoys a spectacular view of the north Michigan Avenue skyline, including the John Hancock Center. And it is difficult to get food any fresher—the staff picks vegetables to order on the spot.

City Farm is an initiative from the Resource Center, a nonprofit organization more than thirty years old that gathers food scraps from area restaurants and converts them to compost. With all that compost heaping up, growing food was a natural next step. Founder Ken Dunn created a way to nurture a green space in the heart of the city, providing organic vegetables for the neighborhood and a number of posh restaurants. He does this to further his interest in social justice by providing jobs and fresh food to people in underserved areas.

City Farm, at its essence, is a portable farm designed to grow food on formerly vacant lots. Currently located along the Clybourn corridor near what used to be the infamous Cabrini Green housing project, City Farm makes the best use of vacant space until long-term development plans fall into place.

Working with Chicago city officials, Resource Center identifies property expected to be vacant for at least five years. Then the work of creating the farm begins. First, workers lay a barrier to prevent anything below from leeching into the plants, like chemicals from demolished construction. Then they spread literally tons of compost, three feet deep, and in go the seedlings. When the property is ready to be developed, City Farm simply moves to another block nearby.

City Farm grows garlic, arugula, chard, and seemingly countless varieties of vegetables, but it is best known for its dozens of varieties of heirloom tomatoes. Luscious, wrinkly Brandywines, along with petite, striped Green Zebras and Giant Oxheart (which are indeed heart-shaped) arrive at restaurants such as Lula Café, Frontera Grill, and Vie, individually wrapped in newspaper to prevent any bruising of the perfectly ripe orbs. Patrons can drop by the farm stand onsite, open Saturday mornings and Tuesday and Thursday afternoons, and often any time staff or volunteers are present tending the farm.

Average age of American farmers: 57

City Farm's financials paint an interesting picture about the challenges of such operations. It sold an admirable $60,000 in vegetables in 2008—remarkable, given the small two-acre site—but its operating budget exceeded $100,000. Without the support of donors, this type of food production would not be possible.

The situation, as with a lot of small-scale agriculture, may always be tenuous. Says Ken Dunn, "We rely heavily on tomatoes. If there's a rainy year where tomatoes don't thrive, we fall behind."

61st Street Farmers' Market

Founded 2008

20+ vendors

Saturdays, May through December

61st Street between Dorchester and Blackstone Avenues

A large city is perhaps the clearest illustration of the dichotomy between the haves and have-nots. In some Chicago neighborhoods, houses sell for tens of millions of dollars. In others, often not too far away, more than 60 percent of residents are on some kind of government assistance. Making good food more accessible to all is a challenge.

The Chicago city markets and the Green City Market both accept LINK cards, the electronic cards through which people redeem food assistance benefits from SNAP, the Supplemental

Nutrition Assistance Program, formerly known as food stamps. The 61st Street Farmers' Market, another independent market in Chicago, has found a way to take assistance a step further by obtaining a grant that doubles the amount people can spend.

The 61st Street Market is an ideal venue in the sense that it draws from the affluent Hyde Park neighborhood and its University of Chicago crowd who can afford the fresh food prices, which ensures a good bottom line for market vendors. It also serves the Woodlawn neighborhood, where more than 50 percent of residents are on public aid. The vibrant market typically has more than twenty vendors, including **Ellis Family Farm**, **Tomato Mountain**, **Faith's Farm**, **Genesis Growers**, **Mick Klug Farms**, **Mint Creek Farm**, and **Stamper Cheese Company**. Another highlight is **Blackstone Bicycle Works**, which provides bike services for shoppers.

With the grant program—funded by the Wholesome Wave Foundation—eligible residents receive a $25 match for every $25 in SNAP coupons they are eligible for, essentially doubling the fresh fruits and vegetables they can afford.

Market manager Dennis Ryan is one of the fortunate who seem to look ever young. Tall, slim, and freckled, his excitement is palpable as he talks about bringing good nutrition to an underserved area. He brings with his eagerness some solid experience. He spent time in the Peace Corps, then worked for a decade with large insurance companies before deciding his future was in food. He earned a culinary degree at Kendall College, a professional culinary school in Chicago that emphasizes sustainability, managed the Green City Market, then came on board with Experimental Station, the not-for-profit organization that maintains the 61st Street Market.

The initial matching funds grant from Wholesome Wave came about through old-fashioned networking. Ryan was talking with a long-time advocate of local farmers, chef-partner Paul Kahan of Blackbird, Avec, The Publican, and a few other restaurants at last count. He told Ryan, "You should talk to my friend Michel Nischan." Nischan, best known as chef of The Dressing Room with partner Paul Newman, had started the Wholesome Wave Foundation in Connecticut to address

Michel Nischan, Wholesome Wave Foundation

the dichotomy in food accessibility in his home state. In just a few years the foundation had mounted similar programs in fifty-five communities across the United States. In addition to helping people in need, it has established markets in areas that might not have them.

"Anything we do has to work for the farmers *and* the shoppers," Ryan says—meaning if the farmers cannot sell enough to make their numbers, they will not consider it worth the trip. Conversely, if the shopper cannot afford the food, there would be no market.

This is exactly what happened at one market started at the Greater Galilee Missionary Baptist Church in Chicago's underserved North Lawndale neighborhood. Church members recruited two farmers to come to the church parking lot after Sunday services, but after a five-week pilot they found that not enough members could afford the price. The church did not have an electronic benefits transfer (EBT) that functions as a debit card for SNAP beneficiaries. Since most church members were low income, even discounted prices were too steep.

Wholesome Wave Foundation
Matches Food Assistance Funds

A common trait of restaurant people is that they get things done. Michel Nischan is one of those achievers. He has had success with restaurants, books, and consulting gigs, and he cooks on The Victory Garden on public television, showcasing bounty from the garden. In short, he is the kind of person who makes the rest of us feel tired. But clearly Nischan has energy to spare when it comes to a topic he feels passionate about.

"I was frustrated that local food was a white-tablecloth movement," he says, adding that white-tablecloth restaurants only represent 10 percent of all restaurants. When he was a chef at Fleur de Lis in Milwaukee in 1981, Nichan drove fifteen to twenty hours each week to source local food.

"It was a lot of work," he says. Later in his career, sourcing food directly from farms was easier in Connecticut, where many farm mortgages were paid off and widespread commodity farming had not taken hold.

He looks at the issue from two sides, from the point of view of the underserved communities, but also from the perspective of keeping small growers in business. Nischan comes from farming roots in Missouri along the Mississippi River. He tells about working on his grandfather's farm for a month every summer, and how the growth of large agriculture conglomerates changed the fabric of the culture there. He heard their personal histories.

"There were 'farm widows' from World War II, where the husband and sons didn't come home. Large agribusinesses would buy the farm but let the widow stay in the house. Buying those small farms would give them rights to the local co-ops, and they'd dump their crops for very low prices to force others out. Then they could buy those other farms at rock-bottom prices."

Nischan's mission dates back to his childhood, but it was early in the current century when he made it a larger part of his life. A 2007 session sponsored by American Farmland Trust featured Daniel Imhoff, author of *Food Fight: A Citizen's Guide to the Farm Bill*. Nischan was in the audience when Imhoff reviewed a pie chart outlining farm bill expenditures. As always, the conversation went to a discussion of how to divert some of the $3.7 billion that went to twenty thousand cotton growers. "That's a lot of money per farmer," says Nischan. But for small fruit and vegetable farmers to wage a battle against big agribusinesses seemed futile, an uphill battle at minimum. Nischan says, "I'm looking at this pie chart at the front of the room, and I raised my hand and said, 'What's that big yellow piece of the pie?'" Food stamps. At the time, $30 billion were going to food assistance. By 2009 the figure had increased to $60 billion. Food assistance accounts for about two-thirds of the farm bill budget.

Gus Schumacher, former undersecretary of the United States Department of Agriculture and local food advocate, was also attending. "So Gus and I locked ourselves into the handicapped washroom so no one would bug us and started talking about how to make this work. We realized if we could devote even five percent of the amount to fresh local food, the difference would be massive." Nischan and Schumacher founded the Wholesome Wave Foundation to create a matching funds program as an incentive for qualified people to shop at farmers' markets.

Daley Plaza market, one of more than twenty operated by the city of Chicago

And incentives are needed. Of the six thousand farmers' markets registered with the USDA, more than 90 percent are in affluent areas, says Nischan. Which makes some sense, as small farmers do not have the economies of scale to offer deep discounts. Thus, it is typical that the more affluent population with the discretionary income can pay the higher prices for small-scale production. But Nischan is out to prove that it does not have to stay this way.

"It's great to know that underserved communities can be the underdog hero in this story. Our next objective is to get low-interest loans for farmers with thirty to one hundred acres because those are the size farms we'll need more of."

Logan Square Farmers' Market

Founded 2005

45 vendors

Sundays, June through
October

Logan Boulevard at
Milwaukee Avenue,
Chicago

The Logan Square Market has a festive atmosphere in
a neighborhood that is hip and gentrifying. At **Lucila's
Homemade**, you'll find *alfajores,* sandwich cookies filled
with *dulce de leche,* a caramel spread native to Lucila
Giagrande's home in Argentina. After you polish off a
crepe at **Cook Au Vin**, get a baby cone at **NiceScream** for
a dollar. Provenance sells cheese. Score sour cherries from
Noffke Family Farms and vegetables from **Earth First
Farm, Iron Creek Farm, Radical Root Organic Farm,** and
M's Organic Sustainable Farm. Videnovich Farms sells
gorgeous vegetables, including peppers of every size and
color. Buy bread from **Golden Rise Bakery**: it will go great
with a generous spread from **Rare Bird Preserves**, where
Elizabeth Madden cooks up small batches of lovely combinations like apricot almond and ginger rhubarb.

Chicago Botanic Garden Farmers' Market

Founded 2008

First and Third Sundays,
May through October
(outdoors); first
and third Sundays,
November and
December (indoors)

1000 Lake Cook Road,
Glencoe

Although not technically in Chicago, the Chicago Botanic
Garden is a resource for many city dwellers. For years the
Botanic Garden has hosted weekly chef demonstrations
in the Regenstein Fruit and Vegetable Garden to help
guests learn about seasonal cooking. A farmers' market
was a natural extension.

King's Hill Farm sells a diverse range of foods, from
vegetables to eggs to honey, all raised in Mineral Point,
Wisconsin. **River Valley Ranch Farm**, a mainstay at many
area markets, sells fresh mushrooms, plus pickled mushrooms and mushroom pasta sauces. **Faith's Farm** offers
free-range, chemical-free beef and pork from nearby
Bonfield, Illinois. **Green Youth Farm** sells vegetables,
including the most vibrant carrots you will ever see; the
farm also hosts a training program to teach youth about
organic growing.

Farmers' Market Glossary

The Farmers Market Coalition created these definitions to help shoppers understand foods they will find at their local markets.

artisan/artisanal   The terms "artisan" and "artisanal" imply that products are made by hand in small batches.

biodynamic   Biodynamic farming is based on the work of Austrian philosopher Rudolf Steiner. In addition to organic practices such as crop rotation and composting, biodynamic farmers rely on special plant, animal, and mineral preparations and the rhythmic influences of the sun, moon, planets, and stars.

certified farmers' market   Some states offer or require certification of farmers markets to ensure that the products sold are produced by the farmers themselves. As of 2009, these states include California, Nevada, and Texas. Most of the nation's producer-only farmers' markets establish their own rules and methods of ensuring product integrity at the local level.

certified naturally grown   Certified Naturally Grown (CNG) products are certified by an independent nonprofit organization (not USDA) as having been produced in approximate accordance with national organic standards, a program involving fewer paperwork requirements and lower certification fees for farmers than the USDA's National Organic Program.

closed herd   Implies that all animals are bred from the original herd. No animals are purchased to incorporate into the herd.

conventional   Refers to standard agricultural practices that are widespread in the industry. Can (but does not necessarily) include use of pesticides, synthetic fertilizers, "mono-cropping," antibiotics, hormones and other chemical approaches. Conventional farming in the United States may also include the use of genetically modified organisms (GMOs).

dry aged   Meat that is dry aged is hung in a temperature- and humidity-controlled room for a period of weeks to develop flavor and tenderness. Most commercially available meat is wet aged by vacuum packaging.

dry farmed   Produce grown using a tilling technique that seeks to retain moisture in the soil and to minimize or eliminate the use of irrigation.

EBT Electronic Benefits Transfer (EBT) is an electronic system that allows participants in the Supplemental Nutrition Assistance Program (SNAP) to authorize transfer of their government benefits from a federal account to a retailer account to pay for fresh foods. A growing number of farmers' markets are equipped with the technology to accept SNAP benefits.

free range Free range, free roaming, and pastured imply that a product comes from an animal that was raised unconfined and free to roam. "Free range" claims on beef and eggs are unregulated, but USDA requires that poultry have access to the outdoors for an undetermined period each day.

farmstead cheese Farmstead cheeses are made by the same people who farm the animals producing the milk—in other words, a cheese that is "from the farm."

GAPs Good Agricultural Practices (GAPs) are a collection of recommended principles for on-farm production, post-harvest processing, and storage of food that all reduce risks of microbial contamination.

genetically modified organisms (GMOs) GMOs are plants and animals whose genetic makeup has been altered to exhibit traits that they would not normally have, like longer shelf life, different color, or resistance to certain chemicals. In general, genes are taken (copied) from one organism that shows a desired trait and transferred into the genetic code of another organism. Genetic modification is currently allowed in conventional farming.

grass fed The diet of grass-fed animals consists of freshly grazed pasture during the growing season and stored grasses (hay or grass silage) during the winter months or drought conditions. Grass feeding is used with cattle, sheep, goats, and bison.

heirloom Heirloom crop varieties, also called farmers' varieties or traditional varieties, have been developed by farmers through years of cultivation, selection, and seed saving, and are passed down through generations. Generally speaking, heirlooms are varieties that have been in existence for a minimum of fifty years.

heritage A term applied to breeds of livestock that were bred over time to be well-adapted to local environmental conditions, to withstand disease, and to survive in harsh environmental conditions. Heritage breeds generally have slow growth rates and long, productive lifespans outdoors, making them well suited for grazing and pasturing.

humane If an animal product is labeled "humane," it implies that the animals were treated with compassion. "Certified humane" means that the animals were allowed to engage in their natural behaviors; raised with sufficient space where they are able to lie down, have access to shelter, and receive gentle handling to limit stress; and given ample fresh water and a healthy diet without adding antibiotics or hormones. Not all "humane" claims are regulated.

integrated pest management (IPM) A pest-management strategy that aims to reduce the use of chemical pesticides through careful monitoring for actual pest threats. Pesticides are applied in such a way that they pose the least possible hazard and are used as a "last resort" when other controls are inadequate.

locally grown Food and other agricultural products that are produced, processed, and sold within a certain region, whether defined by distance, state border, or regional boundaries. The term is unregulated at the national level, meaning that each individual farmers' market can define and regulate the term based on its own mission and circumstances.

naturally grown/all natural USDA guidelines state that all "natural" meat and poultry products can only undergo minimal processing and cannot contain artificial colors, artificial flavors, preservatives, or other artificial ingredients. The claim "natural" is otherwise unregulated.

no antibiotics Antibiotics are given to animals such as cows, hogs, sheep, and chickens to prevent or manage diseases. "No antibiotics" implies that a farmer does not administer antibiotics to his or her animals.

no hormones Hormones are commonly used in the commercial farming of animals such as cattle to speed the growth rate or increase milk production. Some of these hormones are natural, some are synthetic, and some are genetically engineered. If a ranch or product professes "no hormones," this means that they do not engage in these practices. Hormones are not allowed in raising hogs or poultry.

no spray/pesticide free   While a farm may not be organic, "no spray" or "pesticide-free" indicates that no pesticides, herbicides, or fungicides have been applied to the crop at any point in its production.

no till   A method of reducing soil erosion by planting crops without tilling the soil, which may rely on herbicides to control weeds.

organically grown/certified organic   All products sold as "organic" must meet the USDA National Organic Program production and handling standards. Certification is mandatory for farmers selling more than $5,000 of organic products per year and includes annual submission of an organic system plan and inspection of farm fields and processing facilities to verify that organic practices and record-keeping are being followed.

raw   Foods such as milk, cheeses, cider, vinegar, sauerkraut, or almonds that have not been pasteurized (heated) to a minimum of 145 degrees Fahrenheit. In the United States, raw-milk cheeses are required to be aged for sixty days. In some states, sales of raw milk are prohibited.

seconds   Produce that is bruised, blemished, over-ripe, misshapen, or otherwise deemed unfit for regular sale. Seconds, for cooking or canning, are often available in large quantities and at lower prices.

SFMNP   The Senior Farmers Market Nutrition Program (SFMNP) provides eligible low-income seniors with coupons that can be exchanged for fresh fruits, vegetables, honey, and herbs at farmers markets. Funding for the SFMNP is provided by the USDA Food and Nutrition Service to states, U.S. territories, and federally recognized Indian tribal governments.

sulfured / no sulfur   Many dried fruits are sulfured with sulfur dioxide (SO_2) or metabisulfate to keep them from oxidizing during and after the drying process. This preserves their original color and acts as a preservative. Unsulfured fruits are often dark brown in color.

sustainable agriculture   Farming that is socially just, humane, economically viable, and environmentally sound. The term is unregulated.

transitional   Farmers must practice organic methods for three years on a given piece of land before the products harvested from that land can be sold or labeled as organic. "Transitional" is an unofficial term means that the farmland is in the midst of that transition period toward organic certification.

vegan   Foods with this label contain no animal products such as meat, dairy, eggs, gelatin, or honey.

vine ripened/tree ripened   Fruit that has been allowed to ripen on the vine or tree. Many fruits that are shipped long distances are picked while still unripe and firm; they are later treated with ethylene gas at the point of distribution to "ripen" and soften them.

WIC cash value voucher (CVV)   WIC Cash Value Vouchers, or its equivalent state-sponsored name, allow farmers to accept WIC fruit and vegetable checks at farmers' markets by enrolling them as limited WIC vendors.

WIC FMNP   The Women, Infants, and Children Farmers Market Nutrition Program provides coupons to eligible low-income women who are pregnant, breastfeeding, and/or caring for children up to age five who are found to be at nutritional risk. Coupons are used to buy fresh fruits, vegetables, and herbs at farmers markets. Funding for the WIC FMNP is provided by the USDA Food and Nutrition Service to states, U.S. territories, and federally recognized Indian tribal governments.

wood-fired oven bread   Breads baked in an oven made of brick, clay, or sod that is heated by burning wood.

This glossary is for educational purposes only. It does not endorse or discredit any of the practices included herein. Created by the Farmers Market Coalition in partnership with the Marin Farmers Markets and the Center for Urban Education about Sustainable Agriculture (CUESA).

Red HAVeN 3.00

Redhaven peaches hail from
South Haven, Michigan

Michigan

My home state of Michigan may always be the Automobile State, no matter what the highs and lows of that industry are. It is the birthplace of the assembly line, and American carmakers are still based around Detroit. Men of a certain age—like my father—remember when new models traveled to dealerships shrouded in canvas so they could be unveiled all at once.

And yet many people do not know that Michigan also is a food powerhouse, second only to California in terms of crop diversity. It is known predominantly for its fruit belt along the western side of the lower peninsula: the climate there, with proximity to Lake Michigan, makes it particularly suited for fruit production. The state has small, diversified farms in just about every county.

The southwest corner of the state was a hotbed of fruit creation for decades. Under the guidance of Stanley Johnston, head of Michigan State University's experiment station in South Haven from 1920 to 1969, the first cultivated blueberries started right here beginning in 1930. Today the state is number one in blueberry production, providing 35 percent of the country's stock. Johnston may be most famous, however, for cultivating the Redhaven peach. Most people do not know that this flavorful gem was part of a family of eight "Haven" peaches designed to span a longer season and thus deliver more fresh fruit to citizens and more profit to farmers. Many of these, like Fairhaven, Cresthaven, and Sunhaven, are not household words, but Redhaven continues to bear the standard for southwest Michigan. Lately, the Flamin' Fury peach has burst on the scene, cultivated by Paul Friday of nearby Coloma.

Southwest Michigan, where I spend most weekends, is still famous for its fruit, and a number of fruit crops are commissioned by companies like Welch's for grape juice and Gerber for baby food. It is also a place of hidden treasures like **Pleasant Hill Farm**, where farmer John Van Voorhees and Joan Donaldson farm forty acres of organic blueberries with a team of oxen named Henry and Buck and fertilize only with compost tea. Their pick-your-own operation is open in mid- to late summer. The Rubel, Blue Crop, and Jersey blueberry bushes were planted on the farm in the 1930s, possibly as part of Stanley Johnston's initiative, and they are still popular for their flavor and versatility. In a few years patrons will be able to pick peaches as well—Donaldson and Van Voorhees planted one hundred peach trees in 2011. Their farm has the added bonus of being off the grid. Their power comes from wind and solar resources, and they use a wood stove to heat their house.

Around the "corner," a few miles away at **Evergreen Lane Farm and Dairy**, Tom and Cathy Halinski maintain about forty La Mancha goats and make four kinds of goat cheese, welcoming visitors to buy from their farm store. A few miles farther on, Samuel Fleming of **Fleming Farm** grows organic vegetables and has carved out an additional niche by tapping hundreds of maple trees for the wood-fired maple syrup he sells at the Saugatuck, South Haven, and Holland farmers' markets. He partners with Doug Hamm at **Songbird Acres** to evaporate the syrup at Doug's sugar shack. Songbird Acres also keeps one hundred laying hens for eggs sold from the farm. Hamm has about one hundred ISA

Brown laying hens who have free run of a generous henhouse and access to the outdoors. If a circling hawk makes the "girls" nervous, they can duck for cover underneath many of the outbuildings or head back into the henhouse, which is closed up at night against nocturnal predators like raccoons. The farm has a handful of setting hens who incubate the eggs to maintain the flock.

These are the southwest Michigan farms I visit when I need blueberries, cheese, or eggs. This kind of farming community used to be the norm but has become less so with the advent of large-scale, industrial farms and increased development. But there is hope. In many areas, biodiversity is returning, and younger farmers are entering the field. There are bustling markets in South Haven, Holland, St. Joseph, and, most recently, Fennville.

Downtown Ann Arbor Farmers' Market

The downtown market in Ann Arbor's historic Kerrytown district was founded in 1919 and is considered Michigan's longest-running continuous farmers' market; with more than 150 vendors, it is certainly among the largest.

Rick Bayless, the acclaimed chef we met in the Chicago chapter who has made it a mission to help growers, gravitated to this open-air market when he was a graduate student at the University of Michigan in the 1970s, and he credits his experiences here with setting him on his farmer-friendly path. This market, with its permanent shelters for vendors and shoppers, is large and busy, so it is best to go early and bring your patience. **Frog Holler Farm's** Ken King has been selling organic vegetables at the Ann Arbor market since 1972. King's wife and three sons are partners in the farm, which first was a 165-acre wildlife sanctuary. The **Goetz Family Farm** represents multiple generations growing on a farm that has been in the same family for more than one hundred years.

Founded 1919

150 vendors

Wednesdays and Saturdays, May through December

Saturdays, January through April

315 Detroit Street, Ann Arbor

They need two tables to display their vegetables. **Esther Knapp** sells vegetables and plants; seek out **Amos Coblentz** for eggs and jams. Score some Dick's Pretty Good Garlic at the **Dyer Family Organic Farm**—they grow more than forty varieties of garlic—and try their garlic scapes early in the season.

Farmers at the Downtown Ann Arbor Market

» Jeff Nemeth is part of a family operation that currently spans three generations in Milan, about twenty miles south of Ann Arbor. He shares eighty acres with his grandfather, who operates the **Alex Nemeth and Son Orchard**. His mother, Joanne, spearheads the greenhouse operation and has control over any crops they start from seed, and Jeff is in charge of the direct-sow crops like green beans, peas, and sweet corn. He estimates the non-orchard crops at **Nemeth's Greenhouse and Farm** to be about twenty to thirty acres.

Chefs appreciate the melons started by Joanne and harvested by Jeff. His prized watermelons include old-fashioned varieties like Red Sugar Baby, which he nicknamed cannonballs because they are small and dark; other popular watermelons include Athens, Super Sweet, and Classic. Both Nemeths, the thirtysomething Jeff and almost-eighty-year-old Alex, sell at the Ann Arbor markets, often with Jeff's four-year-old daughter in tow.

Michigan produces more blueberries than any other state

Nemeth's orchard dates to 1931 when Alex's father launched the family business. Alex tells about how his father was "a farmer, and a hungry one" when he discovered an opportunity with a bank-owned orchard. At the height of the Great Depression, banks could not hope to move many foreclosed properties. The banker wanted the orchard maintained and therefore gave Alex's father the opportunity to work the orchard and reap the profits. After two years he was able to buy the orchard. Alex remembers attending the Ann Arbor market with his father as a young boy.

A number of things have changed, though. "Back then we only sold four varieties of apples, and they were chosen because they had tough skins and could last the winter," Nemeth says. Those traits are no longer desirable, given today's cold storage facilities, and thus those varieties, like Wealthy and Duchess, are no longer in demand. But there are four varieties from his childhood that still show up at market tables, including Jonathan, Winesap, Red Delicious, and the early Transparent, a good apple for cooking and baking pies.

» Although not a farmer, John Savanna of **Mill Pond Bakery** counts as a true food artisan. He came to baking at age thirty-three, and only years later he discovered it was in his genes. "I knew early on that food would be my life's work," he says. After working a number of years in the natural foods business, he started Mill Pond Bakery in 1980. About fifteen years later his wife looked into the family history, and Savanna's Aunt Jeannette sent photos of the family bakery in Langres, France. Savanna's American father and French mother married in France in the aftermath of World War II. They split when he was a child, and Savanna grew up with his father near Detroit, not knowing about his baking roots.

It turns out that his grandfather, a native of Alsace, had relocated to the town of Langres and bought the Boulangerie Henri IV in the 1920s. The 150-year-old oven still bakes eight hundred to a thousand baguettes each week for a nearby boys' school.

Savanna discovered another coincidence. It turns out that his French relatives still sell bread at the market in Chaumont every Wednesday and Saturday, the same days that Savanna's wife, Colleen, sells at the Ann Arbor market. Savanna's adult children, Jessica and Jonah, are also involved in the business.

Gabe Blauer works with John Savanna at Mill Pond Bakery

» Dwight Carpenter, of **Carpenter's Organics** in Allen, transitioned from conventional growing to organic in the 1980s. "The main reason," he explains, "is that when I was younger, I did all the spraying and ended up with a brain tumor." Carpenter's father overhears his son's story and grumbles his dispute regarding the chemical cause. Regardless, the benign tumor was treated successfully, "But I didn't want to poison anyone," Dwight says.

The change to organic production was not easy. He decided to grow tomatoes hydroponically in his 4.5-acre greenhouse and subsequently saw his yield drop 90 percent, from thirty pounds per plant to three. After experimenting and trying new organic fertilizer and additional irrigation, the yield increased to eight pounds per plant, so he believes he is on the right track. He also grows tomatoes outdoors, along with about thirty other kinds of vegetables in his seventeen-acre garden. His tomato of choice is Mountain Pride, which he prefers for its great flavor. Carpenter has fifty-six acres overall, with a lot of woods, perfect for the three hundred free-range ISA Brown laying hens, reddish brown birds that look like a diminutive Rhode Island Red. Small as they are—about six pounds, compared to the eight- to nine-pound Rhode Island Red—they eat less and are more economical to keep. "But their eggs are huge," says Carpenter.

>> Deb Lentz and Richard Andres of **Tantré Farm** in Chelsea sell at the market and also operate a 350-member CSA (Community Supported Agriculture) chapter. Andres bought the fifty-acre farm in 1993, and since the land had been used for hay production (and therefore not farmed with chemicals), he did not need transition time to grow organically. He grew vegetables in bulk for the local food co-op and also worked as a timber-frame carpenter. Andres and Lentz, who was an elementary schoolteacher, met and married. When their daughter was born, Lentz stayed home, and the two were able to launch their CSA.

Lentz grew up on a beef farm in Minnesota. In another classic example of how inspiration comes from unexpected connections, Lentz tells about traveling to hear her father speak at a farming conference. There they heard John Peterson of Angelic Organics describe his CSA model and took his philosophy to heart. Tantré Farm's "maybe someday" happened in 2001 with thirty members. Lentz and Andres grow nearly one hundred kinds of vegetables, as well as tree fruit and berries. Their recent additions are kiwi—"We found a hardy northern variety," Lentz says—and the endangered paw paw, as well as a native plum, *Americanas prunas,* that requires little maintenance and ripens in the fall.

Goats, chickens, cats, and an Australian cattle dog round out the farm's residents. And Tantré Farm also maintains six Guernsey cows for a cow share program, where members buy a share of the cow and then pick up their raw milk at the farm.

Cow share programs typically operate quietly because selling raw milk is prohibited for food-safety reasons. Bacteria such as salmonella, listeria, and *e. coli,* which might be present in raw milk, are eliminated through heat-treatment methods like pasteurization. All milk sold commercially or directly from a farmer is required by law to be pasteurized. Regardless, some people sing the praises of raw milk for health benefits and taste. Enter the idea of a cow share program: because people who "own" cows are entitled to drink the milk their cows produce, farmers offer "shares" of cows. The cost of buying into a cow covers the board, feed, and milking of that cow. The share owner visits the farm to pick up the milk.

Standards for such programs need to be beyond meticulous, which is often what one finds at small operations. There is another advantage to a grass-fed operation, or cows that graze on pasture: at large, conventional dairies, where cows are not fed what nature intended them to eat, cows are in "a perpetual state of diarrhea," according to Lisa M. Hamilton, author of *Deeply Rooted,* a book about unconventional agriculture. Smaller, compact, pasture-based operations—where cows eat the diet they were meant to eat—have the added bonus of being easier to keep clean.

That said, fresh is the watchword of the day. Studies have shown that raw milk can deteriorate faster than pasteurized milk, being bacteria free on Monday and in fully contaminated bloom by Thursday. So it is important to drink fast.

Ann Arbor's Westside Market

Founded 2005

20 vendors

Thursdays, June
through September

2501 Jackson Avenue,
Ann Arbor

Chef Rodger Bowser of Zingerman's Delicatessen and a cadre of volunteers, including market manager Corinna Parker and webmaster Kristin Kelley, started the Westside Market to accommodate increased demand for space at the Downtown Ann Arbor Farmers' Market. "We realized that the downtown market had a waiting list," Bowser notes, "and that there might be an opportunity for an afternoon market across town."

Westside Market has no operating budget aside from in-kind services and is housed in the parking lot of Zingerman's Roadhouse. Because everything, including staff, is donated, the market charges no stall fees to the vendors, making it a more profitable venture for producers who participate.

My market visit was on a windswept day—so windy, in fact, that Corinna Parker spent a lot of time helping vendors tie down their tents.

Rodger Bowser, chef at Zingerman's and founder of Ann Arbor's Westside Market

Zingerman's All Around

If Chicago's Frontera is a culinary microclimate, then perhaps Zingerman's is an inspiration kitchen of sorts, one that advances small businesses focused on quality food. It is often said that the measure of a great chef is how many great chefs come out of his or her kitchen. Those who inspire others to go off and cook well are rewarded with a legacy. Alice Waters comes to mind, the doyenne of local cooking who has assembled an unrivaled alumni community that includes prominent chefs Deborah Madison, Dan Barber, Judy Rodgers, Jonathan Waxman, Jeremiah Tower, and Suzanne Goin.

Zingerman's in Ann Arbor seems to be a "great chef" in the local food movement, inasmuch as this bustling community of businesses has spawned a number of local food enterprises. Ari Weinzweig and Paul Saginaw founded Zingerman's in 1982 to serve full-flavored traditional foods. Zingerman's has expanded from there, with a decidedly local focus: two of its concerns, Zingerman's Creamery and Zingerman's Bakehouse, focus on patronizing local producers. Chef Alex Young went so far as to launch Cornman Farms to produce vegetables for Zingerman's Roadhouse and also to have a more family-friendly schedule for employees.

"Our expansion into these areas has been driven by prospective partners," Weinzweig says. The company's employees are encouraged to bring business ideas forward, always supporting the vision of flavor and tradition. One venture—the Ann Arbor Westside Farmers Market—is not a moneymaker, but it fits into the company's vision nonetheless..

Weinzweig's dark curly hair and Converse gym shoes give the appearance of someone who would be at home in a different era altogether. He tells about how his mother took him to the Democratic National Convention in 1968, the year protesters rioted in Chicago's Grant Park. His casual manner belies the business savvy he speaks fluently. He gives all the credit to his staff, but the staff finds Zingerman's a source of inspiration. Weinzweig clearly has found a place in this world where one can "do good and do well."

Farmers at the Westside Market

» John and Cathie McLaughlin of **McLaughlin Meats** produce beef from shaggy Highland cattle on land that John's grandfather bought in 1932; it was a dairy operation until the 1950s. One reason the McLaughlins decided on Highland cattle is because they originated in the Scottish highlands and, with their heavy coats and thick hides, they are ideally suited to the Michigan climate. Add good mothering instincts and longevity, and this breed has the traits for a beef herd that can thrive. The meat is lean, well marbled, and flavorful.

» Paul Howell and Amanda Smith from **Dragonwood Farm**, a two-acre operation with sixty laying hens, offer eggs, flowers, and vegetables. The gorgeous eggs come from equally beautiful chickens from the Aracauna, Welsummer, Delaware, and Speckled Sussex breeds.

Paul Howell and Amanda Smith of Dragonwood Farm run their operation on two acres

» Peter Klein was working in marketing when he discovered his favorite fruit farmers were retiring. After looking at his options and developing a business plan for an orchard venture, he decided, "This was a *really bad* idea." Bad idea or not, he did what most fruit lovers only dream of—he bought the retiring farmer's eighty-acre orchard. Now under the brand of **Seedling Fruit** in South Haven, Klein added heirloom fruit varieties, including some listed on Slow Food's Ark of Taste. His orchard is currently up to about seventy-five hundred trees. (More on Slow Food later.)

As a true marketer in every sense, Klein looks for ways to differentiate himself from other fruit growers. One staffer who liked to bake began experimenting with different apples and coined the term "the holy trinity of pie apples," referring to the trio of Northern Spy, Golden Grimes, and Idared. Indeed, the magic combination yields a flavor and texture that is impossible to duplicate with grocery store Granny Smiths. Shoppers can pick up a bag of holy trinity apples already mixed rather than buying a bag of each. Those little touches make the difference in a farmer's success, particularly one who does not have value-added products to sell.

Seedling Fruit, South Haven, Michigan

Value-added products are those taken a step beyond their natural state: grapes into wine, fruit into jam, milk into cheese. These products command a much higher price compared to the raw ingredients, and they can make great contributions to a farmer's bottom line. Klein has embraced the value-added idea by creating a line of jams, mostly, he says, so he would "have something to sell in the winter." Next he installed a cider facility and introduced a line of varietal ciders like Jonagold, Mutsu, and Golden Delicious, along with flavored ciders enhanced with tart cherries or cinnamon. These are a contemporary interpretation of traditional products. His ciders are now carried in Whole Foods, which decentralized its buying policies to allow store managers to feature more local foods. His hard cider hit the market in 2009.

Peter Klein of Seedling Fruit is a marketer turned orchardist

A visit to Seedling Fruit in southwest Michigan's orchard belt is a feast for the senses. The "new" house is at least one hundred years old, and the older house, just a few yards away, is much older but still sturdy. Outbuildings include three barns—one is a "cooler" set up for cold storage, another the cider house, and a third the headquarters for Seedling's annual harvest fest, a party that draws guests from as far away as Chicago to enjoy grilled food and tour the orchard. Workers' quarters are nearby.

"Melon-dramatic" Salad

Rodger Bowser, chef, Zingerman's Delicatessen

In addition to his work with the Ann Arbor Westside Market, Rodger Bowser still makes time to cook. On paper, this recipes sounds delicious; in the bowl, it is a captivating feast for the eyes, with its vibrant melons mixed with pale green cucumber punctuated with the white salty cheese. The simple flavors make an intriguing mix of cool refreshment and a hint of heat from the onions. Bowser uses red and yellow watermelon from Jeff Nemeth, one of the first farmers to sign up for the Westside Market, and Manouri cheese, a Greek goat's milk or sheep's milk semi-soft cheese made from whey that is drained from feta production. He recommends using any firm, salty, crumbly cheese from your area.

"The salt marries well with the sweetness of the melon, and the colors really pop," Bowser says.

SERVES SIX TO TEN

2½ pounds Yellow Stars or Sunshine watermelon, cut into 1-inch chunks

2½ pounds Red Sugar Baby watermelon, cut into 1-inch chunks

2 medium cucumbers, peeled, halved, and seeded, cut into ½-inch moons

1 pound Manouri cheese, cut into ½-inch dice

1 medium red onion, peeled and thinly sliced

1 bunch mint

juice and zest of 3 lemons (about ¾ cup juice)

½ cup olive oil

Place melon chunks in a large bowl and sprinkle with lemon zest. Gently toss. Add cucumber, cheese, onion, and mint. In a small bowl, whisk together lemon juice and olive oil. Just before serving, pour over salad and gently turn to combine.

Northport Farmers' Market

Founded 2008

6 vendors

Fridays, June through
September

102 North Rose Street,
Northport

The Northport Farmers' Market is one of six in Leelanau County, the peninsula that forms the pinky finger of Michigan's mitten-shaped Lower Peninsula. This intimate market unfolds in front of the train depot on the shore of Northport Bay. A standout vendor is **Bare Knuckle Farm**.

Jess Piskor and Abra Berens are two effervescent, twentysomething farmers who cut their culinary teeth working at Zingerman's while attending the University of Michigan. Berens cooked with Rodger Bowser, who founded Ann Arbor's Westside Market with an army of volunteers. Jess worked at Zingerman's Deli, then made cheese at Zingerman's Creamery, and also worked at Cornman Farms, which grows vegetables for Zingerman's Roadhouse.

When they decided to go into business, an opportunity was waiting on Piskor's grandfather's farm in Northport. Bare Knuckle Farm is tucked into a little hollow in the midst of an orchard, predominantly of tart cherry trees. The two-acre garden lies in a lower area where trees would not thrive, making it a great place to grow vegetables.

The pair received heartwarming support from friends. "We had thirteen friends come to help paint the barn," says Berens. Now with a freshly painted, red-striped yellow barn, they are planning the next project: installing hoop houses.

They took an intuitive approach to choosing what to grow. "I look for vegetables that have a good story," says Piskor. "I want tomatoes that are true to what they are supposed to taste like." "And we plant what we like," says Berens. "I like Swiss chard so we planted a lot of that."

Bare Knuckle Farm sells at two markets in Leelanau County: Northport and Sutton's Bay. Because their farm is located so close to the markets, which open at a leisurely

9 A.M., Piskor and Berens typically pick in the morning and arrive at the market with produce just hours out of the ground. The Bare Knuckle table at the Northport Farmers' Market shows a distinct flair for merchandising. Vegetables are stacked up in wooden crates and vintage metal dishware; scallions are tied with string. Miniature tomatoes are measured out in diminutive brown paper sacks. Prices are listed on slate chalkboards set up on lawn chairs. Deep green and purple string beans tumble together in a wooden box. The farm's painted-wood sign—"Since 2009"—is propped on crates below.

"I've never felt so appreciated," says Piskor. "People are always telling me that they enjoyed the beets. People here love beets." Berens chimes in, "People stop me in the grocery store to say thanks for being here."

The pair spends the off-season honing other food skills, with Berens off to cook and bake in Chicago at Floriole Bakery, another business that started by selling at a farmers' market, and Piskor to New York to work in a cheese store. And they think ahead, planning for future seasons. Geese, ducks, and chickens feed in an area slated for the hoop house next season. The birds will then move down the row, and later around the perimeter of the farm, fertilizing as they go to amend the soil that will eventually end up in crop rotation. Pigs are in the plan for pork to serve at farm dinners.

Abra Berens and Jess Piskor of Bare Knuckle Farm

Berens credits Rodger Bowser for being her mentor. He coaxed her to train at Ballymaloe Cookery School in County Cork, Ireland, in part because the course is three months rather than two years. Students learn key techniques and leave with a solid foundation that is open to further interpretation depending on where students want to go from there. In many ways it is also the best place to train as a farmer/chef. Ballymaloe founder Darina Allen is staunchly connected to the land, to the point that the first recipe students learn is compost. Allen believes chefs must be soldiers at the forefront of the effort to reinvent our food culture.

Allen states her point of view with passion. "We've come to view cheap food as a right, and it's not a right." She advocates that food professionals should take up their pens and write about why small-scale production is the lifeblood of every culture, and that chefs in particular play a role in working with growers as well as educating their clientele.

After Ballymaloe, Berens spent an additional three months in London as an intern with Neal's Yard Dairy, the café at Petersham Nurseries, and Stickleton cheese, makers of a raw-milk cheddar in the tradition of Stilton, which transitioned to pasteurized milk in the 1970s. "My training gave me confidence to walk into a kitchen, but not too much confidence. I can still ask, 'How do *you* make mayonnaise' rather than thinking I know everything," she says. Her dream is to have a café at Bare Knuckle Farm. There is no reason to doubt that she will one day.

In addition to embracing Zingerman's devotion to local ingredients, Berens also benefits from its entrepreneurial vision. The team has visions of a family of businesses, including perhaps Bare Knuckle Wild (a foraging arm), in addition to the restaurant, as well as a bed and breakfast. For the farm, there are plans to replace some of the orchard trees whose production has declined (tart cherry trees need to be replaced every nine years or so). And since their microclimate is about two weeks behind Sutton's Bay just to the south, they get a slightly lower price for their fruit: it is a straightforward case of supply and demand—the growers who get the fruit on the table before everyone else can command a higher price before the abundance hits.

And so to diversify, Berens and Piskor plan to add tree nuts such as filberts and black walnuts, as well as uncommon fruits like paw paws, which are native to the region but are almost impossible to find. They plan to nurture wild apples as well. Their overall goal is to foster a regional cuisine. "I get bristly when people talk about French food being better, or even when people talk about *salsa verde*. It's green sauce," says Berens.

Berens and Piskor talk about working in a region where people are aghast at a $50 donation for a multicourse dinner, whereas that would be considered a bargain in a metropolitan area like Chicago. Of three

Bare Knuckle Farm Pear and Carrot Mostarda

Paul Virant, Vie

At a recent fundraising dinner for Bare Knuckle Farm, Chef Paul Virant paired a pear and carrot mostarda with a raclette cheese from the Leelanau Cheese Company, Bare Knuckle's neighbor to the north. The sweet pears and carrots get a vigorous kick of mustard, making it a great foil for roasted or boiled meats, as well as a condiment for a cheese course.

1 pound firm pears (about two or three), such as bosc—peeled, cored, and diced

½ pound carrots (about three medium), peeled and sliced julienne style

¾ cup sugar

½ cup water

2 tablespoons pear or cider vinegar

½ teaspoon salt

½ teaspoon cracked black peppercorns

½ teaspoon fennel seed

1 tablespoon black mustard seed

1 tablespoon Dijon mustard

1½ teaspoons Coleman's dry mustard powder

Bring sugar, water, vinegar, salt, pepper, fennel seed, and all three mustards to a boil in a large saucepan. Add carrots and cook until *al dente*, just barely tender. Add pears and continue cooking until pears are soft. Remove pears and carrots with a slotted spoon and cook liquid to 218 degrees (test with a candy thermometer) to thicken. Replace pears and carrots and bring to a boil. Remove from heat and transfer to a tightly covered container. Store in the refrigerator for up to a month. Recipe can be doubled.

"If I am
what I eat,
then I'm fast,
easy, and
cheap."

—BUMPER STICKER

dinner parties Bare Knuckle has hosted, almost every ingredient has come from the farm. For the first they bought rabbits from nearby Bunny Hop farm. For the others, they served chicken and duck from their own flock, and supplemented only with celery, parsley, and blueberries from neighbors, as well as butter, lard, and suet. Berens goes on to say that better pigs yield better lard, indicating that quality shows up in the flavor at every level of food production, something she says she learned cooking with Paul Virant at Vie, in his Michelin-starred restaurant in Western Springs, Illinois, in the offseason, when Bare Knuckle Farm is dormant.

Downtown Saginaw Farmers' Market

Founded 1910; since 1992 in current iteration

18 vendors

Mondays, Wednesdays, and Fridays, May through October; plus Saturdays, July through October

507 South Washington Avenue, Saginaw

Saginaw, about eighty-five miles north of Ann Arbor along I-75, paints a somewhat down-to-earth picture of local food production. The city's records date the market to 1910, although there was a hiatus from the 1950s to the 1970s, as with so many city markets that lost their audience to supermarkets.

The city of Saginaw's fortunes, even more so than in other parts of Michigan, have been tied to the automobile industry. As General Motors declined, so did the city. The market switched locations several times over the years, as people were required to drive through increasingly troubled neighborhoods to get to the market. Low turnout is the kiss of death for farmers' markets, but that seems to have been resolved with the current downtown location.

The Downtown Saginaw Farmers' Market now opens four days each week, in part because the area is considered a food desert that is not served by any supermarket.

Area residents have few options for buying fresh food, making this market a rare choice. And while most markets have worked hard to put processes in place to accept SNAP benefits, WIC coupons, and Senior Nutrition benefits, this is a market where people actually redeem those benefits.

The energy at the Saginaw market is upbeat and dynamic, with a deep sense of community and tremendous diversity mixing all ethnicities and ages. Cars jockey for parking places in the crowded parking lot, navigating around the potholes. Close to lunchtime a line forms for **Dude's Gumbo**, a Louisiana-style gumbo served over rice. Longtime patron Mary Margaret Fletcher says she comes because it reminds her of when she worked for a vendor thirty years ago for sixty-five cents an hour when the market was located at the Michigan Central Depot on Genesee Avenue.

Market master Paul Corrion performs a number of duties onsite, everything from offering directions to helping patrons redeem their SNAP benefits. One theme throughout farmers' markets is that organizers are eager to help people use all available food assistance to make the market accessible to those who might not otherwise be able to afford it. He is strict about the starting time, with one exception: police officers get to shop early.

Farmers of the Saginaw Farmers' Market

» Shelley McGeathy of **McGeathy Farms** is both executive director of the market and a flower farmer in Hemlock, a town about twenty miles west on highway M-46.

» Shelly and Matt Harrell of **Timm Family Farm** grow melons, pumpkins, and a variety of vegetables on land that belonged to Shelly's grandmother. They tell their favorite story about a woman who wanted a melon for her mother and asked for guidance about picking a ripe one. She came back the next week, to say her mother had not "tasted a melon like that since the Melon Lady was at the fairgrounds." The Melon Lady was Shelly's grandmother, who had sold produce at the farmers' market decades before. A shopper chimes in, "This is the best leaf lettuce I've ever had." The

Shelley McGeathy

Shelly and Matt Harrell of Timm Family Farm, famous for their melons

Harrells—and probably farmers everywhere—are gratified when clientele compliment the superior flavor of their food.

» Like many farmers, Jim DeWyse of **DeWyse Farms** is a career changer, but with a family history in farming. After retiring from the Central Foundry (a division of General Motors), he is now growing food where his grandfather farmed. He is proud to say that his grandfather never "worked out"—referring not to exercise but to the fact that his grandfather supported his family from farming and never had to get a job off the farm.

» **Lighthouse Bakery** sells about sixty sweet-potato pies at the market every week. **Guevara Produce** grows Hispanic vegetables, including lots of hot peppers on various plots scattered around the region. **Briggs Orchard** grows paw paws, other tree fruits, and nuts. **Super Bee Apiaries** offers honey products, and **Black Dog Farm** sells heirloom tomatoes and other vegetables.

Meridian Township Farmers' Market

- -

45+ vendors

Saturdays, May through October; Wednesdays, July through October

5151 Marsh Road, Okemos

Outside Lansing is a farmers' market that creates significant buzz. **Macs Centennial Farm** and **Wildflower Eco-Farm** provide vegetables. **Thomas Organic Creamery** is the place for yogurt and ice cream, plus beef and hot dogs. **Country Mill Farms** offers apples, cider, and doughnuts, the perfect fall trifecta. **Owosso Organics** sells vegetables, herbs, and plants. **Greenbush Farms** sells goat cheese. **Spartan Country Meats** serves up chicken, turkey, and rabbit. **Hannewald Lamb Company** is the place for lamb, and the **Fresh Lake Whitefish Company** sells wild-caught whitefish, trout, walleye, and perch. **Craig's Hilltop Honey** has the sweet stuff. Visit **Stone Hearth Breads and Bakery** for the baked goods. The **Purple Carrot Food Truck** has soups and sandwiches on site.

Detroit Eastern Market

"The Eastern Market is the soul of Detroit, not just the stomach," said market president Dan Carmody. It is a massive collection of five sheds, covering five city blocks if you include parking spaces. On Saturdays it draws around forty-five thousand visitors. What many visitors do not see is that the area is also a regional wholesale hub for grocery stores and restaurants and teems with trucks from midnight to 5:00 A.M. The market's infrastructure provides an ideal location to boost sales of regional foods because it has facilities for storage and processing.

Shed Two, with the signature "Eastern Market" carved across the front, was built in 1891. The area was declared a historic landmark in 1977 and several years ago transitioned from a city-run concern to operating under the guidance of the nonprofit Eastern Market Corporation, which created a master plan to make the market the center for fresh and nutritious food in the area. Vendors must grow 100 percent of their offerings and be Michigan based or grow within a hundred-mile radius of the market. To make its fresh food accessible to all residents, the market participates in the electronic benefits transfer, as well as the Double Up Food Bucks from the Fair Food Network.

One vendor, the **Detroit Agricultural Network**, may be a unique organization. For a modest membership fee, it will test garden soil and provide seeds and seedlings for gardeners. If the soil test reveals no harmful substances, such as lead, gardeners have the option of selling their surplus later in the season. Member Lacey Story gardens on a double lot in Detroit's Rosedale neighborhood and publishes the Canning Tomatoes blog. "For only ten dollars they tested my soil, and sometimes I donate my extra greens to sell at the market," Story says. Members have the option of pocketing the proceeds or donating back to the network.

Founded 1891

250 vendors

Tuesdays and Saturdays, year round

2934 Russell Street, Detroit

One of the gems is **Hampshire Farms**, a rare vendor of grains like wheat and spelt, milled into flour, as well as oatmeal, popcorn, and dried beans grown on their 240-acre farm. Randy and Shirley Hampshire's daughter Amalie and son Brandon are part of the operation, which is certified organic. In 1991 they built a wood-fired oven and offer yeast-free, whole-grain sourdough breads. They also sell eggs from pasture-raised chickens.

Vegetable vendors abound, including **DeMeulenaere Farm**, **J & S Farms**, and **Holtz Farms**. Look for pork from **J & M Farm**. **Zen Organics** is known for its nut butters.

Carmody calls the Eastern Market "the last of its kind and perhaps the first of a new generation" because its structure harkens back to the flurry of activity when small farms were the norm, and because it is ideally suited to help remake the area's food system.

In addition to being the state's largest farmers' market, the Eastern Market has the distinction of serving as a food hub for many city residents who do not have cars or access to a supermarket. The USDA defines a food hub as "a centrally located facility with a business management structure facilitating the aggregation, storage, processing, distribution, and/or marketing of locally/regionally produced food products." In other words, a food hub functions as an evolution of a farmers' market model, something along the lines of how early grocery stores operated when they had relationships with local or regional producers.

Jim Barnham is the food hub team leader for USDA's Agriculture Marketing Service. His team has created a working group that seeks to better understand how to foster the success of food hubs by joining forces with five other U.S. government agencies, including Rural Development and Food and Nutrition Service, as well as a few not-for-profits partners.

"Detroit is a poster child for food hubs," says USDA's Wendy Wasserman. "They have a big physical site with a processing facility." These resources can help farmers move their food to eager buyers, from individual farmers' market shoppers to large-scale food service operations.

Detroit's Eastern Market also is the focal point for a program designed to get fresh, healthy food into the kitchens of underserved eaters. The Fair Food Network pioneered its Double Up Food Bucks program at the Eastern Market and saw an increase in food assistance buying by 368 percent by offering bonus tokens to people using their SNAP benefits. Today it operates at more than forty farmers' markets across Michigan, with plans to reach about eighty in the next few years.

Fulton Street Market, Grand Rapids

The Fulton Street Market in Grand Rapids is the city's oldest and largest, located in the Midtown neighborhood. When it comes to assigning booth spaces, the market has a well-defined pecking order: farmers first, then other food vendors (like bakers), then artisans and crafters. Find the **100 Acre Woods Honey Farm** for honey, **Blueberry Heritage Farm** for blueberries and cranberries, and **Bob Alt Farm** for berries and pumpkins. **Ham Family Farms** has vegetables, including vibrant purple broccoli, and **McKeown Brothers** and **Platte Family Farm** are both known for luscious sweet corn. Stop by **Brickyard Farms** for multicolored organic carrots, and **Nels Nyblad Orchard** for apricots and cherries. The Salvation Army hot dog cart provides job training for high school students. Free speech areas on either end of the market are ideal for street performers and political candidates.

35+ Vendors

Tuesdays, Wednesdays, Fridays, and Saturdays, year round

1149 Fulton Street, Grand Rapids

Muskegon Farmers' Market

Founded 1884

50+ vendors

Tuesdays, Thursdays,
and Saturdays, May
through December

700 Yuba Street,
Muskegon

The Muskegon Market was the oldest continuously operating market I found. Market master Lori Gomez-Payne said that in the 1940s, when most markets were dying off, the Muskegon Market thrived due to foundry workers who migrated to Michigan from the South during World War II. These Southerners had an agrarian heritage and gravitated to the market, keeping it active, whereas in other areas, supermarkets proliferated.

Here is where you find an abundance of vegetables from **Boersma Greenhouses**, **Jean's Produce**, **D&M Farms**, **Kathy's Produce**, **Rio's Produce**, **Witt Brothers**, and **Hoffer Greenhouses**. Find orchard fruit at **Leutzinger's**, **Dain's Orchard**, and **Afton Orchard**. **Funny Farm** sells organic produce. You will find plants from **Heiss Hillside Flowers**, **JW Greenhouses**, **River's End**, **Bishop Farm**, and **Jobey's Greenhouse**. **Maple Creek Sugars** serves up honey and syrups. Get dessert from the **Maple Island Pie Company**. Get meat from **Creswick Farms**. **Laughing Tree Brick Oven Bakery** makes its own yeast and bakes in a wood-fired oven fueled by locally cut wood from stoneground Michigan flour produced by **Ferris Organic Farm**. Their dense bread sells out every week.

Because Michigan is nearly surrounded by the Great Lakes, fish has been part of its native food culture for thousands of years. Amber Mae Peterson, wife of a fourth-generation fisherman, recognized an opportunity to extend her family's business by selling direct to consumers. She staked out a space at the Muskegon market because a storefront location would be prohibitively expensive, and now she sells fresh and smoked Lake Michigan whitefish as **The Fishmonger's Wife**. She shows up at the market wearing a floppy fisherman's hat with the brim turned up, looking every bit the part of a high-seas commercial angler, circa 1900.

Peterson processes her fish at a rented kitchen. She cleans and fillets the fish by hand, in part because even a used fillet machine can run $30,000. These challenges to growth explain why small producers are strapped to accommodate demand. And demand there is— The Fishmonger's Wife typically sells out by 10 A.M.

City of Holland Farmers' Market

Eaters Guild Farm, situated in the Black River watershed south of Holland, is a USDA-certified organic farm, operating chemical free since the 1970s. It offers chickens and a wide variety of vegetables, including asparagus and tomatoes. Grassfields Organic Cheese offers a selection of raw milk cheeses, including the occasional "my apolocheese," tasty mistakes available on a limited basis. Visser Farms dates to 1902 and sells dozens of vegetables, from radishes and lettuce in spring to pumpkins and potatoes later in the season. Samuel Fleming of Fleming Farm sells maple syrup evaporated over a wood fire. Other vendors include Sunrise Orchards, Cosgrove Orchard, Dreyer Farm, Stephenson Farms, and Boetsma Produce. Westview Farms specializes in lovely hydrangeas and flowering shrubs. Visit the food court for Ray's Tamales, Lady Liberty Foods, and Hot Diggity Dog.

Founded

45+ vendors

Wednesdays and Saturdays, May through December

150 West Eighth Street, Holland

Ohio

Ohio is known for rolling hills, rich soil, and a deep agriculture history. The state presents a unique mix of markets located in urban alleys, in quiet neighborhoods, even in a national park. And Ohio ventured early into cottage laws, which allow food artisans, like bakers, to incubate businesses by selling at open-air markets. The best way to get to know the farmers and food producers in Ohio is to go shopping.

Cuyahoga Valley Countryside Conservancy

Since 2007

40+ vendors

Saturdays, May through October

Cuyahoga Valley National Park, Peninsula, Ohio

Beth Knorr is market manager for Countryside Conservancy's market at Howe Meadow, tucked into Cuyahoga Valley National Park

A visit to this farmers' market in the heart of a national park is worth the drive alone. A light fog clings to the treetops on an early September morning, the leaves just starting to turn. To reach the market, drivers weave through the Cuyahoga Valley National Park, past a misty pond, a gathering of midcentury ranch houses, then rolling countryside newly crisp with an early autumn chill. Arriving at the Cuyahoga Valley Countryside Conservancy Market in Howe Meadow, they are directed to the parking area by a National Park Service ranger in full uniform, including the signature flat hat. A century-old brown barn marks the entrance, a reminder of the agrarian heritage of the valley. The market itself is nestled in a clearing of trees, vendors arranged in a large open square with green space in the center for picnicking. The weather will be warm enough for shorts once the sun is over the tree line, but for now the farmers wear fleece hoodies and knit caps.

The Cuyahoga Valley National Park flanks the Cuyahoga River, which connects Cleveland and Akron. This rolling area affords a distinctly rural feel on thirty-three thousand acres in between two of the state's busiest cities. It also provides farmers with affluent city shoppers who come to either of the Countryside Conservancy markets, the one in Howe Meadow (in Peninsula, Ohio, at the heart of the park) and another on the grounds of Stan Hywet Hall and Gardens in Akron, at the estate of F. A. Seiberling, founder of the Goodyear Tire and Rubber Company.

Market manager Beth Knorr explains that the Howe Meadow market is ideal for this setting because the park was established to protect the agriculture nature of the region. In addition to attracting diverse producers from the area, three farmers have sixty-year leases right in the national park. This is one of the more compelling elements of the Countryside Conservancy. Growers submit business plans for producing food sustainably, outlining growing practices focused on conservation. A board decides whether to grant a lease. The park maintains farmstead houses and barns, and rents have been characterized as more than reasonable. When accessible farmland is getting more rare, this idea is a way to nurture farmers by giving them a solid start without the need for a large mortgage.

In 2009 Knorr was honored with the first Local Food Hero award from the Ohio Department of Agriculture, given to an individual or organization that promotes and implements local food systems. Knorr was recognized for bringing electronic benefits transfer to the market to allow shoppers to use their food assistance, and for working with Akron County to provide extra funds to people on food assistance.

Farmers at Cuyahoga Valley Countryside Conservancy

» "It's my goal to live out the lease," says Daniel Greenfield of **Greenfield Berry Farm**, who is five years into his sixty-year lease. With a doctorate in education, he may seem an unlikely farmer at first glance, until we learn that his specialty has been environmental ethics and that his grandparents, Russian Jewish immigrants, were farmers. At age thirty-seven he ventured into farming for the first time.

Once he discovered the Countryside Conservancy program, Greenfield sought out the proper training and became master gardener through the Ohio State University extension service in Summit County. Proposals need to demonstrate an understanding of the restrictions and limitations of operating a farm in a national park: respecting wetlands, for instance, as well as buffer zones and historic structures.

Greenfield lives on a farmstead with a house and barn about 150 years old, and although the buildings have been updated with modern amenities, he's required to maintain a historical feel. "I can't paint purple polka dots on the barn, for example." The buildings have been maintained and upgraded with modern heat and plumbing. Greenfield's white house is reminiscent of Grant Wood's painting

American Gothic, with the addition of powder blue shutters on the gothic revival peaked windows.

Of the twenty acres in his parcel, Greenfield has about ten under cultivation—some with perennial crops like berry bushes, and others for annual vegetables, giving him plenty of room for crop rotation. The Greenfield vegetable CSA has forty members who receive a discount on berries, which is predominantly a pick-your-own operation.

Greenfield's crops are certified through Certified Naturally Grown, a nonprofit organization that describes itself as tailored for small-scale farms that sell directly to consumers.

"They're a grassroots organization where farmers inspect other farms, although anyone who visits my farm will see there are too many weeds for it to not be organic," says Greenfield. He echoes what many small farmers say, which is that the USDA national organic program is prohibitively expensive for small operations, adding that many of the rules were written for big producers.

During the long, chilly months, Greenfield participates in a monthly book club. Most fellow members are farmers, and the books they read have an agrarian slant, with authors like Michael Pollan, Joel Salatin, and Wendell Berry. Berry's book of essays *Bringing It to the Table* was the April book, the last before the growing season break. Each month a half dozen to twenty-five readers gather, many times at Greenfield Berry Farm, for spirited conversation.

Daniel Greenfield of Greenfield Berry Farm also hosts an agrarian book club

"Every once in a while we get our torches and pitchforks going, but most of the time it's a reason to get together and enjoy some wine," says Greenfield. "We tend to give people a hard time if they don't bring Ohio wine." And Ohio wine is not hard to find: Sarah's Vineyard is another farm in the Countryside Conservancy program. The conservancy's executive director, Darwin Kelsey, is a frequent participant.

Greenfield Agrarian Book Club Reading List

With nine book club members in farming, Daniel Greenfield's book club leans toward agrarian titles:

Bringing It to the Table by Wendell Berry
The Omnivore's Dilemma by Michael Pollan
The Essential Agrarian Reader Edited by Norman Wirzba
Everything I Want to Do Is Illegal by Joel Salatin
Small Farms Are Real Farms by John Ikerd
America's Food by Harvey Blatt
Living at Nature's Pace by Gene Logsdon
In Defense of Food by Michael Pollan
Organic, Inc. by Samuel Formartz
Animal, Vegetable, Miracle: A Year of Food Life by Barbara Kingsolver

» Deanna McMaken of **Rose Ridge Farm** is a rare find. She and her husband are the fifth-generation farmers on land that has been in her family since it was homesteaded in 1820. That year, James Monroe was president, and fewer than 10 million citizens lived in the Union's twenty-three states. It was in 1820 that the Robertson homestead was registered in Carroll County, and it is on that land that Deanna was born and where she and her husband David McMaken raise organic beef.

The McMakens want their farm to be symbiotic, for all the systems to work together in harmony, and for the food produced there to be grown without chemicals. Of the 450 acres in the family, Rose Ridge comprises about 225. Within that acreage, eighty acres are used for pasture, seventy for cultivating feed for the cattle, and the remaining are woods.

Deanna and David McMaken of Rose Ridge Farm

The McMakens came to farming later in life, taking over from Deanna's father, Dean Robertson, in 1992 after retiring from careers as music teachers. Robertson transitioned the farm from a more diverse operation of pigs, chickens, horses, and cows to a more specialized operation focused on beef. "We took it a step further to focus on organic production and direct marketing." At Rose Ridge, the McMakens produce Hereford cattle, maintaining between twenty-five and thirty-five head at a time. They breed the cows themselves and raise calves for about twenty-four months, significantly longer than the average ten to twelve months for commercial beef.

McMaken says that Herefords are bred for good health, a mothering instinct, and for not requiring as much feed to gain weight. Other breeds, particularly commercial breeds, are now bred for early maturation, making it easier to bring them to market faster. It makes sense that if you feed an animal for an additional year, that the beef from that animal will cost more. Flavor, nutrients, animal welfare, and a healthy environment are bonus points in favor of the extra cost.

The combination of the breed, the longer growth time, and a diet of pasture grasses, alfalfa, and sweet clover, augmented with oats, spelt, barley, and rye result in the superior, subtle marbling in Rose Ridge beef. McMaken credits her nearby processor for helping to make her product a success. The farm is certified organic by OEFFA, the Ohio Ecological Food and Farm Association.

The house where the McMakens live was built by her great-great-grandfather. "The house was pretty much falling down, but we rebuilt it," she says. And the house where McMaken was born and grew up is not far away. The 1920 two-story foursquare had a front porch and its own generator. There is also an early vintage bank barn, where a long slope—or "bank"—leads up to big doors to accommodate farm equipment.

One of the greatest challenges for beginning farmers today is access to quality farmland. That is one factor earlier farmers did not have to worry about. Generations ago, the government set out to settle the country and put measures in place to distribute land to citizens. Today, these measures are considered controversial because they distributed land recently cleared of native Americans and in some cases illustrated the struggle between slave and free states.

The Land Ordinance of 1785 put in place a standardized system of land surveying, ending most boundary disputes. For decades, land was sold for around one dollar per acre, a stiff price at the time. Almost eighty years later, in 1862, the Homestead Act was signed by President Abraham Lincoln. This was a better deal for future farmers, because now they were able to obtain land for free. But it was part of a plan to distribute land in smaller parcels, which would discourage slaveholding—common in the vast plantations in the South.

Individuals could claim 160 acres, and if they lived on the land for the next five years and improved it by building a dwelling and growing crops, they could apply for a deed by providing proof of residency. Union soldiers could deduct time served in the Civil War from the residency requirements. Despite the favorable price point, clearing land and establishing a farm this way was not an easy task. Congress ended the practice in 1976 by passing the Federal Land Policy and Management Act, although it left provisions to continue homesteading in Alaska through 1986.

» At **Curly Tail Organic Farm** in Fredericktown, Ohio, Ed and Beth Snavely raise organic pork. Ed Snavely says he transitioned to organic food production during what has come to be known as "the hog crisis" in the mid-1980s. He remembers how "pork dropped to eight cents a pound, and I decided I couldn't do it anymore." He put his confinement equipment up for sale. After transitioning to organic hogs, his take went from $30 a hog to $80, making his business sustainable. Now he raises Tamworths, a rare, red pig known for positive mothering and milking qualities, and Berkshires. "I keep about a hundred head total, at various ages," he said.

Snavely was a Slow Food Terra Madre delegate twice. He recalls the welcoming "pomp and circumstance" but looks to more local organizations for information and guidance, citing OEFFA, Countryside Conservancy, and Innovative Farmers of Ohio as great resources. He also feels challenged working with restaurant chefs, who prefer only premium cuts like tenderloin, pointing to the need for more education about how to eat well using the whole hog. The farmers' market is a good place to balance demand, where Curly Tail is known for delicious sausage patties and nitrate-free bacon, which come from lesser cuts of meat but still deliver on taste.

Ervin Miller with Alex Dragovich of Mud Run Farm

» The Cuyahoga Valley Countryside Conservancy Market also boasts stellar baking, including short-bread from the **Great Lakes Baking Company**, bread from **Breadnik**, and pastries from **Summit Croissants**, all of which pair nicely with house-roasted coffee from **Crooked River Coffee Company**. Alex Dragovich of **Mud Run Farm** offers grains in addition to chickens and eggs from a farm he works with a team of draft horses.

» And Jeff Brunty of **Brunty Farms** is bringing back the Buckeye chicken, with support from the American Livestock Breeds Conservancy (ALBC). Brunty's adventure in egg production began at age thirteen, when he made a bargain with his grand-mother that if he cleaned her old barn, he could use it to raise chickens.

Expecting the short attention span of a teenager, she agreed. Brunty spent that May and June cleaning the barn, and by July he bought seven hens at auction. By the time he was eighteen, his egg business boasted three hundred chickens. By 2010, at the ripe age of twenty-three, Brunty had a decade of experience and three thousand laying hens. And in 2010 he hatched his first nineteen Buckeye chickens. Brunty credits the Countryside Conservancy and Darwin Kelsey for connecting him with the ALBC.

American Livestock Breeds Conservancy: Saving Buckeyes and Mulefoots

When preparing for the nation's bicentennial to be held in 1976, organizers at Old Sturbridge Village and Plimouth Plantation, the living museums in Massachusetts, wanted their farm exhibits to be historically accurate. Records showed that the earliest settlers had Milking Devon cows, so the organizers set out to find some. They came up empty.

The hardy Milking Devon is a deep ruby brown color with broad white horns. It originated in the seaside area of England, making it a perfect cow for the New England climate, and eventually even the oxen of choice for the Oregon Trail. But by the 1970s, producers were focusing on fewer traits, like giving a lot of milk or maturing in record time.

One reason many breeds have fallen out of favor is their multipurpose attributes. A cow might be good for milk and good for meat, but not exceptional for either. The same goes for chickens like the Buckeye, which is considered a good meat chicken and good egg layer, neither of which makes it attractive for mass production.

Where the Milking Devon was concerned, breeders began to choose between selecting for milk or meat, until the original breed was almost extinct. But a few producers persevered, and now the American Milking Devon breed numbers about four hundred head, up from fewer than one hundred at its demise. It is a breed unique to the United States. Yet even after decades of effort, the American Livestock Breeds Conservancy still lists its status as critical. As with so many preservation measures, success takes time and work.

Today the ALBC works to preserve more domestic livestock and poultry breeds at risk of being lost. They catalog more than 150 breeds of heritage cattle, pigs, sheep, goats, horses, asses, rabbits, chickens, ducks, geese, and turkeys. Preserving species diversity is important, not only from a historical perspective, but also from a food security standpoint. For example, most commercial meat chickens share the same genetic makeup. Imagine if a disaster jeopardizes that population—an epidemic disease, perhaps—and that chicken is no longer viable. Genetic diversity ensures a food supply that has longevity and stability. Another advantage, of course, is a variety of tastes to appeal to the increasingly curious American palate.

This brings us to the effort in Ohio to save the Buckeye chicken, which the ALBC lists as critical: fewer than five hundred breeding birds remain, with five or fewer breeding flocks, and it is globally endangered. Jeannette Beranger is a Buckeye breeder who also manages the research and technical programs at ALBC. She says that Buckeyes are personable, even friendly to people, have quite an active behavior, and, because of the quality meat and good egg laying, they make ideal backyard chickens. Brunty Farm, one of the growers at the Countryside Conservancy Market, has taken up the standard and now produces these birds.

The ALBC is also working to save the Mulefoot hog, one of the breeds produced by New Creations Farm in Chardon, Ohio. Aside from having delicious meat and good fat content (making them desirable to chefs), the breed lends itself to small production because it has a gentle disposition and good mothering instinct. It favors foraging—again, good for flavor—but such innate behavior is the reason it fell out of favor when industrial production increased in favor of hogs that grew faster in a confined setting.

Its most distinctive trait gives the Mulefoot its name. It has a solid hoof like a mule, rather than a cloven hoof found in most pig breeds. The breed is descended from hogs brought to Florida by the Spanish in the 1500s, which were eventually crossed with Berkshire and Poland China pigs to be larger.

Darwin Kelsey is executive director of the Cuyahoga Valley Country-side Conservancy, which operates the markets at Howe Meadow and Stan Hywett Hall. Kelsey is a big-picture person. He holds in his mind a vision for remaking heartland food systems, and he believes that a long view is necessary. This visionary brings not only foresight to Ohio, but also a whole lot of personality. He speaks to the need for more local farmers and points out how to encourage growers. "In 1950 things were different. About one in ten people were involved in food production. Now it's one in fifty," he says.

"So how do we look at a local scale? The Northeast Ohio Fund for Economic Future calculates that we spend $8.5 billion on food every year. We don't grow even 1 percent. If we want to produce 10 percent of our food, that's $850 million worth of food. How many farmers will we need?"

Kelsey does the math in his head. "If we calclulate a gross income of $50,000 per farmer, we'll need more than 8,000 farmers." He goes on to describe the task ahead in terms of putting a truly local food system in place. "We've lost the businesses, the infrastructure, the skill set, even the culture," he says. It is not hard to understand that adding so many farmers to a region will not be easy.

In outlining a solution, Kelsey points to Major League Baseball. "If Major League Baseball has thirty teams with forty players each, how will they get twelve hundred players? By getting kids playing ball." To create local food as the new national pastime, one imagines children Little League gardening and farm clubs, but the idea may not be too far off. With the increasing demand for school gardens and better school lunches, fresh food is making its way back to school.

"Somewhere the light bulb has gone off that we need to go into the area we've avoided for at least ten years, and that's public educa-tion," Kelsey says. Encouraging younger people to experience poten-tial careers and to rebuild pathways with teaching centers, says Kelsey, is the key to encouraging more farming. "In my mind R & D stands for rip-off and duplicate," said Kelsey. "There are lots of good ideas out there." In other words, advocates do not need to reinvent the wheel over and over, just identify what is working and roll it out.

Kelsey brings a long agriculture heritage to his point of view. He came from a farming family in upstate New York, at the very top of the Appalachians, and later worked with the American Livestock Breeds Conservancy during its early days, when it operated as the American Minor Breeds Conservancy, and he then went on to work with other nonprofits. While his rich knowledge is certainly an asset, it is his forward-thinking approach that will make the difference in Ohio's agriculture.

Hudson Farmers' Market

30+ vendors

Saturdays, June through October

Clock Tower Green near Main and Church Streets, Hudson

Historic downtown Hudson serves up the perfect locale to stroll the farmers market. The market is on the lush Village Green, where you'll find ice cream socials in the summer and caroling in the winter. Here you'll find fruits and vegetables from **Thaxton Family Farm** and **Weaver's Truck Patch**. Some Hudson vendors have diversified farms that offer meat and produce, like **Sunrise Farm**, which sells vegetables and beef, and **Bluebird Meadows Farm**, which sells pasture-raised pork, beef, and chicken, as well as strawberries, blueberries and blackberries. **Cossel Farmers** is known for their sweet corn, and **Jonathan Smith** sells all types of organic produce, including herbs. **Hattie's Garden** is a vocational program for adults with developmental disabilities. Prepared foods are available from **Posh Pierogies**, **Top Tier Pastry**, **Gaelic Imports**, and the **Great Lakes Baking Company**. **Blue Jaye Farm** sells jams, maple syrup, and honey. People with a sweet tooth come away satisfied. **Sweets by Dilley**, **Kim's Kitchen Creations**, **Crooked River Herb Farm**, **Lyons Market**, and **Beyond Brownies** sell an array of delights. **Hays Orchard** sells fruit as well as apple cider and apple grape juice by the glass, quart or gallon.

One of the standouts is **Gray Fox Farm**, where Meredith and John Poczontek sell eggs from their flock of pasture-fed laying hens and send out a call for people to bring them egg cartons to reuse. They have a diverse flock of heritage breed chickens, including Black Australorp, Golden Comet, Barred Rock, White Rock, Buckeye, green-egg-laying Ameraucana Sumatra, Buff Chantecler, and Partridge Penedesenca, all supervised by a Columbian Wyandotte rooster. Meredith Poczontek said they prefer heritage breeds because "they tend to be more gentle, lay well all year, and can be used as decent stew hens when we process them." In 2011 they added meat birds to the mix, including Yellow, Redbro, and Tricolor, which grow more slowly than commercial breeds and have retained their scratching instinct and take dust baths. "There's something really peaceful and fulfilling to watch an animal in its natural habitat," said Poscontek. "And they taste delicious."

Gray Fox Farm turkeys range from the standard broad-breasted white to heritage breeds Spanish Bronze, Chocolate, and Narragansett. One year their biggest bird weighed in at a whopping thirty-eight pounds. All the Gray Fox birds live on grass in mobile pens, enjoying fresh pasture every week.

Cleveland Shaker Square Farmers' Market

About a twenty-minute drive north of Cuyahoga Valley is Cleveland, home to the Shaker Square Farmers' Market in a stylish urban neighborhood punctuated by a commuter train running through the center. A reggae band performs. The main thoroughfare hums with shoppers laden with canvas bags. A group of highschoolers promote their garden project. A dog rides in a backpack. Navigating the crowd is not for the claustrophobic.

The Shaker Square Farmers' Market is part of the North Union Farmers' Markets, a nonprofit organization that operates seven markets in the Cleveland metropolitan area. At Shaker Square we meet the folks from **Bluebird Meadows** selling pasture-raised beef, pork, chicken, and eggs. **Goodell Family Farm** is a seventh-generation farm specializing in maple syrup; they recently converted a hay field into the USDA's Natural Resource Conservation Service reserve initiative where they planted several

Founded 1995

80+ vendors

Saturdays, April through December (outdoors); Saturdays, January through March (indoors)

13209 Shaker Square, Cleveland

species of trees—half of which are sugar maples, to be tapped for syrup in about twenty years. **Alpaca Meadows** sells yarn and fiber, and sometimes brings alpacas to meet shoppers. The **Humble Pie Baking Company** serves up pies, granola, jams and jellies. **Rittman Orchards** sells fruits plus twenty varieties of squash and other vegetables, and has a U-pick operation at their farm, featuring strawberries, raspberries, apples, and pumpkins. Avid cooks bring their knives to be spiffed up at **Knife Sharpening with Garth**. Buster and Jeanne Woolf of **Woolf Farms** has been an Ohio mainstay since the 1970s and is known in particular for peaches and sweet corn.

The Shaker Square Farmers' Market is where we meet Julia Boehnlein handing out little cups with samples of pulled pork.

Julia Boehnlein offers samples of pulled pork from her family's New Creation Farm

Seven years old, pony-tailed, wearing spiffy specs and an engaging grin, Julia holds up a tray: "Would you like some pulled pork?" Julia is one of seven Boehnlein children, and with siblings Nicolas and Kaitlyn they make up the cutest sampling staff at any farmers' market, ever.

Scott and Kristen Boehnlein of **New Creations Farm** in Chardon, Ohio, started their heritage pork and beef farm as a way to help their children, six of whom are adopted. One daughter, adopted at age two, came into the family sickly and antibiotic resistant. The Boehnleins stopped feeding her antibiotic meat, which "cost a pretty penny at the grocery store," says Kristin Boehnlein. They also worked to restore her immune system with bee pollen and nourishing, chemical-free foods. Five years later she is thriving and taking ballet lessons.

The Boehnleins were convinced, and now they had a reason for going into the pork business: they could raise flavorful, healthy pork and feed their family at a lower cost at the same time. They keep up to forty mulefoot pigs at time on the fifty-seven-acre New Creations Farm, using production methods in keeping with the animal's natural instincts. Pigs have an inborn rooting habit, so they dig and move things around. Shaggy highland cows move in during early spring. Chickens take care of the cow pies by pecking out the nutrient-rich larvae before they have a chance to become bugs, and this practice does double duty by giving the birds a high-protein diet. The process follows a natural order. "We want to take our land back to a heritage farm," says Kristen.

Animal welfare is evident in the Boehnlein's birthing practices as well. When the mother pigs are ready to give birth, they stay in large farrowing pens, twelve-by-twelve-foot rooms with bedding of sawdust and straw. There are no gestation crates, another controversial confinement method used in commercial food production: the crate restrains the mother pig so that she cannot move, and the piglets feed through bars. Crate proponents claim that without the crates the mother would roll over and crush the piglets, but Boehnlein explains that selecting the proper breed eliminates that risk. Mulefoots are good mothers.

Kristen has a natural approach to nutrition as well, and she enlists her children as allies in healthy eating. "Too many parents say no to foods, but they don't explain why. I teach them why certain foods are good for them, and now they're very conscious," she says. Asked what is their favorite vegetable, and each Boehnlein child expresses a different preference: tomatoes, green beans, squash. "My kids love vegetables," Kristen says.

"We wanted to start a business that could involve our whole family," Kristen notes, adding that a family business based on taking care of livestock animals creates a solid work ethic. "Working with animals is a great way to teach kids respect and empathy," she says. If the precocious and charming trio at the Saturday market is any indication, the strategy is working.

Cleveland Clinic Community Farmers' Market

Founded 2008

20+ vendors

Wednesdays, June through October

Carnegie Avenue and East 100th Street (at the Circle Mall on the Cleveland Clinic Campus)

The Cleveland Clinic Community Farmers' Market is also part of the North Union Farmers' Markets. Its location is just outside the Cleveland Clinic Wellness Institute where noted health expert Michael Roizen, MD, is the chief wellness officer in the department of preventative medicine. He boasts a lengthy list of impressive medical credentials, but he is perhaps best known to the average farmers' market shopper as the author of *Real Age: Are You As Young As You Can Be?*—that, and multiple guest appearances on Oprah. The Wellness Institute is one of twenty-six institutes at the internationally renowned Cleveland Clinic.

Elizabeth Fiordalis directs community outreach for the Cleveland Clinic and tells about the origin of the farmers' market: "Our mission is to extend beyond our walls into the neighborhood, because we know that positive change happens in a group, a neighborhood, a community. Hosting a farmers' market is a way to provide an actual benefit rather than just talking about it."

Fiordalis relates stories about the busloads of students and seniors who pull up to the market, about people buying fresh fruit to take up to patient's rooms, about children sampling tomatoes in colors like pink and purple and green, and about teenagers selling salsa they made from ingredients grown in their own salsa garden sponsored by **Green Corps**, a partnership with the Cleveland Botanical Garden.

The most remarkable story she shares is about a group of Bhutanese refugees, more than seven thousand miles from their homeland, who have started farming in the area and selling at the farmers' market. Until recent years these refugees were farming in tropical lowlands at the edge of the Himalayan Mountains. Fleeing persecution and forced labor, they found help through individuals in the community who learned of their desire to continue their farming heritage and steered them toward farmland for lease. Now these immigrants have found a place to practice their craft, and a welcoming market for their prized vegetables.

North Union requires growing practices that ensure the focus on fresh and local. They include low-herbicide methods and integrated pest management, and food must be grown within 115 miles of the site and picked within twenty-four hours of arriving at market. The Cleveland Clinic Market has a distinct advantage for growers. While North Union Markets Executive Director Donita Anderson states one of her goals is to have markets where the farmers will "sell out the truck," this market host goes the extra mile. AVI Foodsystems, the foodservice provider for the hospital, commits to purchasing much of the perishable food not sold by the end of the market. Within a day, the food is served to patients and visitors. In 2008, AVI Food Systems purchased about $15,000 in produce. As they say in the trade, that's a lot of lettuce.

Dublin Farmers' Market

Historic Dublin hosts a charming midweek market that features **Oink Moo Cluck Farms**, **Moffitt Maple Farms**, **Mockingbird Meadows Honey and Herb Farm**, **Speckled Hen Farm**, **Hirsch Fruit Farm**, and **Spring Haven Farm**. **Wayward Seed Farm** is certified organic and grows more than one hundred varieties of food, many of them heirloom. **Blue Jacket Dairy** sells half a dozen kinds of cheese as well as whey-fed pork.

Founded 2009

20 vendors

Wednesdays, May through September

81 West Bridge Street, Dublin

Olde Worthington Farmers' Market

Founded 1987

70+ vendors

Saturdays, May through October

Downtown near the intersection of Routes 23 and 61, Worthington

Worthington's downtown business district draws shoppers visiting **Pleiades Maple Products** for syrup, **Mockingbird Meadows** for honey, **Osage Lane Creamery** for goat cheese, **VanScoy Farms** for hydroponic vegetables, and **H-W Organic Farms** for vegetables. Get baked goods from **Lucky Cat**, **Gluten-Free Expressions**, **Weed Knob Acres**, and **Landrum Cottage**. Purchase well-raised meat from **Cedar Cress Farm Pork** and **Long Meadows Grass Beef**.

Clintonville Farmers' Market

Founded 2003

70+ vendors

Saturdays, April through October

Dunedin and North High Streets, Columbus

This vibrant region of Columbus also serves up a lively farmers' market, which finishes each season with "stone soup" created by the good people at Alana's, a restaurant known for buying from Ohio farmers. Here you will find lovely lettuces and heirloom tomatoes at **Meadow Rise Farm**, grains from **Naomi's Garden**. Shop for fruits, vegetables, and flowers at **Paige's Produce** and **Rhoads Farm**, a local source for vegetables and fruits since 1958. **Rock Dove Farm** is working toward organic certification. **Ochs Fruit Farm** has been in the family since 1872. Bob and Bev Sexten have raised bison on their **Ohio Bison Farm** since 1990. The market boasts a surprising variety of Ohio cheese, featuring farmstead gouda from **Oakvale Farmstead Cheese**, and grass-fed gouda and cheddar from **Jubilee Meadows Farm**, which also offers beef and pastured Berkshire pork. The **Kokoborrego Cheese Company** is Ohio's only sheep's milk cheese maker, part of the **Sippel Family Farm** operation. To complete your farmers' market feast, visit **Patisserie Lallier** for French pastries and desserts, and **P's Kitchen** for pies and other baked sweets. **Dan the Baker** sells European style breads.

Reynoldsburg Farmers' Market

At the Reynoldsburg Market, which boasts the "heart of the harvest," **Black Thai Farm** sells Asian vegetables, and **Mr. Cherry** is particularly known for peaches. Other vendors sell everything from sunflowers to sweet corn to giant juicy melons. Some vendors are able to sell at farmers' markets because of the Ohio Department of Agriculture's cottage law and home-baking license program. These statutes allow home bakers to sell their creations within the state of Ohio without cumbersome licensing fees and costly inspections, as long as they are not potentially hazardous foods. Nicole Fowler of **Sweet Addictions Bakery** started baking in order to send her daughter to Washington, D.C., on a school trip. She obtained a home bakery certificate through the Department of Agriculture.

Founded 2008

Thursdays, July through September

Huber Park, 1520 Davidson Drive, Reynoldsburg

Nicole Fowler of Sweet Addictions Bakery with her husband, Troy

The Path to a Great Grass-Fed Burger

Kevin Caskey is the dad half of the father-son chef team behind Skillet, a casual farm-to-fork Columbus restaurant started in the depths of the great recession of 2009 and still going strong. Caskey hails from Greenfield in Ohio's Highland County, and he credits the vibrant food scene in New Orleans for giving him his start. Perhaps his studies in medicine at Tulane University—which he abandoned to go into the food business—is what drew him to focus on the health benefits of pasture-raised beef. Caskey shops the Pearl Alley Market in Columbus at least twice a week.

Caskey also buys beef from former aeronautics professor Dick Jensen at Flying J Farm, a 250-acre operation in Johnstown, Ohio, with buildings that date to the 1840s, and from Homestead Farm, operated by John and Cathy Baumgardner in New Carlysle. The Flying J Farm posts health benefits of grass-fed beef on its website, stating that it is higher in good omega-3 fatty acids and lower in cholesterol, both great for reducing heart disease, and high in conjugated linoleic acid, recently considered to help fight cancer. These attributes drive many people to consider the higher price for grass-fed beef well worth the cost.

But cooking can be a challenge at first when weekend grill masters slap burgers on the grill, char them black and are surprised by a slight liver flavor. Chef Caskey explains why pasture-raised meat can be a little tricky. "Because the animals are outdoors and moving, the meat does not lend itself to heavy marbling," he said, "and so they need to be cooked a little different. We use different cuts of brisket, short rib and bottom and top round in our burgers, rather than all ground sirloin." The mix of cuts lends a bit more natural fat, resulting in a tender burger. All that's left to do is to broil it to medium rare.

For those of us who buy grass-fed ground beef at the farmers' market, give it a little drizzle of olive oil or ask your producer to put aside a little fat for you to mince up and mix in. Chefs take all meat away from the heat before it reaches the perfect doneness, because meat will continue cooking as it rests, and this is particularly important with a grass-fed burger.

"Meat can increase from six to ten degrees as it rests," says Caskey.

An instant-read thermometer the best tool to help you know when your burger is ready. Medium rare is 130–135 degrees Fahrenheit. Take your burger off the heat when it reaches 125, and it will be tender and juicy.

Columbus Pearl Alley Farmers' Market

Tidy, brick-paved alleys in downtown Columbus transform into a bazaar twice a week. You will find plenty of artisans and artists, and also plenty of places to grab lunch. There are also some great farmers here: stop by **Bergerfurd's Farm Market and Greenhouse**, **Darby Valley Farm**, and **Henson Farms**. **Brigner Ridge** features honey and preserves. **Wishwell Farms** is a fourth-generation farm that brings luscious strawberries, a wide variety of vegetables, and pepper relishes. **J Squared Organics** boasts a beautiful array of soaps and body scrubs.

Becky Barnes of **Honeyrun Farm** near Williamsport is another grower who came from farming roots and is evolving into new directions. Barnes and her brother Isaac keep seventy-five beehives, and Barnes also leases six acres from her father and uncle, who grow corn, soybeans, and wheat on two thousand acres and are in the process of handing the farm down to the next generation.

"Sweet corn wears me out," she says, referring to the weight, which tends to feel even heavier when loading a truck after a warm day. Her three acres of corn will be planted with other vegetables the next season. Her rent is a highly desirable $150 per acre, probably because of the family discount. She grows five varieties of potatoes: Green Mountain, Austrian Crescent, Rosefin Apple, Roman, and German Butterball.

In addition to her presence at the farmers' market, she sells to North Market Green Grocer in Columbus, which has a fresh-bag program, operating something like a CSA. Her restaurant patrons are on High Street: Rigsby's Kitchens, North Star, and Elena.

20+ vendors

Tuesdays and Fridays, May through October

Alleyways behind Broad, High, Gay, and Third Streets, downtown Columbus

Becky Barnes of Honeyrun Farm

OEFFA: Ohio Ecological Food and Farm Association

OEFFA was organic before organic was cool. The Ohio Ecological Food and Farm Association was founded in 1979 and was certifying farms well before the USDA's National Organic Program was in place. In fact, members of OEFFA's staff participated in establishing the USDA organic standards. It is the oldest operating certification group in the country and currently certifies around seven hundred farms in Ohio, Michigan, Indiana, Kentucky, West Virginia, and Pennsylvania.

Certification begins with an application process, which can take up to four months. Each farmer submits an application in the spring identifying crops, acres planted, and expected yield, as well as inputs, water quality and use, conservation practices, and a litany of other elements that affect the organic nature of an operation. After that, the farm is inspected by an independent third party who evaluates the farm against fifty pages of organic policies and procedures.

> "We want people to shake the hand that feeds them."
> —OEFFA

The association also goes to great lengths to educate farmers. The focal point of OEFFA's education program is an annual conference that boasts keynote speakers in the pantheon of organics, like Joel Salatin, whose Polyface Farm in Virginia was made famous in Michael Pollan's landmark work *The Omnivore's Dilemma,* and Chef Ann Cooper, who calls herself the renegade lunch lady and has made it her mission to change the way children eat at school. The conference has 60+ workshops to educate interested parties, from beginning farmers to seasoned veterans honing their craft. Other programs throughout the year target backyard gardeners on topics like composting, and its website features the Good Earth Guide, a searchable database of farmers and foods.

OEFFA also organizes farm tours "to encourage people to shake the hand that feeds them," says Lauren Ketchum, OEFFA's head of member services. Tour participants might be consumers seeking to learn more about food production and producers who want to learn from each other.

Athens Farmers' Market

The Athens Market had humble beginnings with three farmers but now has a stunning variety of vendors. Stop by the **Silver Bridge Coffee Company** and **Crumbs Bakery** first to plot your strategy. For vegetables, choose from **Sayre Produce**, **King Family Farm**, **Firefly Valley**, **Duff Farms**, **Gibson Ridge Farm**, **Barringer Farm**, **Cowdry Farms**, **Adkins Greenhouse**, **Rich Gardens Organic Farm**, **HerbaVore Gardens**, **Murphy's Farms**, **Sassafras Farms**, or **Shade River Organic Farm**. Find meat at **Dexter Run Farms**, **Elk Run Buffalo Farm**, and **Harmony Hollow Farms**, and baked goods at **Golden Acres**, **Heaven's Oven**, **Pie in the Sky**, and **Grandma's Rolling Pin**. You'll find fruit all season long at **Cherry Orchards**, **Gillogly Orchard**, **Bodacious Berries**, **Crumb Strawberry Farm**, **O'Brien Family Farm**, and **Blackberry Sage Farm**. **Crowing Rooster** farm sells duck and chicken eggs.

At **Laurel Valley Creamery**, the happy Jersey cows roam the woods on property that has been in Nick Nolan's family since 1947. **Integration Acres** makes goat cheese, which you can serve in a salad drizzled with their maple pawpaw vinaigrette. **Athens County Master Gardeners** are on site to dish out advice on good growing and environmental stewardship. The **Donation Station** accepts contributions for local food pantries. If you are still lingering at lunchtime, stop at **Avalanche Pizza**.

Founded 1972

100+ vendors

Wednesdays and Saturdays, April through October

1000 East State Street, Athens

Findlay Market

Founded 1852

30+ vendors

Saturdays and Sundays,
April through November;
also Tuesdays, June
through November

1801 Race Street at
Elder Street, Cincinnati

Findlay Market is Ohio's oldest ongoing public market. The outdoor farmers' market is a magnet for shoppers in this historic neighborhood. Get vegetables from **Simpson Produce**, **Ron Roth Produce** and **Niemeyer Farm**, homemade sweets from **1893 House**, and baked goods from **Cake Rack Bakery** and **Blue Oven Bakery**. **Bee Haven** has the honey.

Hyde Park Farmers' Market

30+ vendors

Sundays, June through
October

Hyde Park Square,
Cincinnati

While the Findlay Market is the mother ship in Cincinnati, dating to 1852 and now with its own farm, other smaller, neighborhood markets grace the area as well. One of them is the Hyde Park Farmers' Market, a walkable gem.

Cofounder Judy Williams lived in France and enjoyed the neighborly connections she found at her local open-air market, in addition to the fresh food. When she moved to Cincinnati, she teamed up with former Californian Mary Ida Compton, who also longed for seasonal produce. The two established a market for their neighborhood.

At the market **Fab Ferments** sells more than pickles, offering an array of fermented food using ancient techniques, including kombucha, kimchi, and krauts, and a beverage called kvass. Dan Berger of **Maple Grove Farm** makes maple syrup the old-fashioned way, with buckets and a wood-fired evaporator. Jim Lowenberg

of **Running Creek Farm** waxes poetic about his garlic, which enjoys sun and good soil. He plants thirty-three hundred heads each fall for a June harvest. The farm-based **Blue Oven Bakery** sells twenty-five kinds of wood-fired breads. Rounding out selections are soaps and flowers, plus prepared foods like pasta, pesto, and **Duncan's Delicious Doggie Delights**.

Indiana

Indiana's local food community is so deep, there's an entire book to describe it. *Home Grown Indiana: A Food Lover's Guide to Good Eating in the Hoosier State* is written by university professors Christine Barbour of Indiana University (Bloomington) and Scott Hutchinson of Purdue. The authors remind us that every county in Indiana holds local treasures waiting to be tasted, and that one should look beyond the corn alongside the interstate highway to seek out flavorful foods.

Yet as with other heartland states, or any state with rich soil that has been planted with monoculture crops, the goal of localizing Indiana's food system is not without its challenges. One forward-thinking producer suggests that the state is in a commodity rut and has not been active in helping growers break into new markets. But producers and eaters are clearly leading a charge for small-scale, diverse food production.

Indiana's food culture is deep and rich. It has its own state pie, for instance, and lives up to its reputation as the crossroads of America. Many farmers in southern Indiana count Louisville, Kentucky, as the nearest metropolis, and growers in the northwest part of the state make almost daily treks to Chicago to deliver their food.

Bloomington Community Farmers' Market

Founded 1975

95 Vendors

Saturdays, April through
November

Showers Common, 401
North Morton Street,
next to Bloomington
City Hall

Tuesdays, June through
September

6th and Madison Streets

Bloomington, home to Indiana University, has an outdoor market with a distinctly festival-like flair and a mix of official and impromptu entertainment. There is a covered stage with a full schedule of performers every Saturday, and improvised performance spaces crop up in different areas around the market. One young man sits on a stone wall playing guitar. Step dancers clomp on wooden pallets, with a band rocking out behind them and children dancing along in front. Across the way a violinist plays classical music. Somehow the performers do not interfere with each other, and all contribute to the sense of occasion. A portion of the market is devoted to prepared foods, and a dozen or more shoppers relax along a knee-high wall with a pastry or fresh tamale from **Feast**, catching up and soaking up the atmosphere.

The current location of the market is next to the city building and features permanent awnings that shelter the farmers. Farmers pull right up to their stalls and sell directly from their trucks. Forty eager shoppers wait, canvas bags in hand, to buy corn from the back of a particularly popular truck. The line did not diminish over several hours.

Although it seems that most farmers' market shoppers are environmentally aware, this was the one where I spotted no plastic bags. Apparently these shoppers never forget the canvas bags at home or in the trunk of the car. Some shoppers carry big bags of popcorn tucked under their arms. The fragrance is prominent, a reminder of Indiana's popcorn heritage: indeed, Indiana native and Purdue graduate Orville Redenbacher launched the nation's most popular popcorn brand from Valparaiso in the 1970s.

Farmers of the Bloomington Community Farmers' Market

>> Jeff Hartenfeld of **Hart Farm** has been selling at the Bloomington Market for more than thirty years and also wrote a book with his wife Jennifer Meta Robinson, *The Farmers' Market Book: Growing Food, Cultivating Community*. Not surprisingly, Robinson thinks of community first when thinking about her farmers' market. "I find that people want a social supplement in addition to a nutrition supplement," she says. "Going to the farmers' market is more difficult than driving to the supermarket, so people are coming for more than the food." It's clear that people are enjoying the social experience as they linger, canvas bags full. "Every day people live in their own worlds. The market is a place where their worlds intersect with others," says Robinson.

Jeff Hartenfeld of Hart Farm is one of the first vendors at the Bloomington Community Farmers' Market

The Bloomington market is in a university town, and Robinson is not the only faculty member who sells there. Robinson lists her fellow faculty: "We have a biologist selling honey and a geologist selling wild gathered things." Others sell beef and vegetables. Robinson and her husband sell fresh-cut flowers and nursery plants such as raspberries, horseradish, and rhubarb.

She has had her students conduct ethnography projects wherein they observe how people interact at the market. These new visitors to the market are often charmed by how friendly the market is, or how they sometimes get things for free; other times they are surprised at people handling the food in a casual manner.

Because Hartenfeld has been selling at the market since 1976, the year it opened, Hart Farm is one of only four with the most seniority. Vendors receive a point for every day they sell, and those with the most points get prime locations. His station is in the center of the market with a good view of the main music stage.

Marcia Veldman is the Bloomington Market manager and also a grower

>> Marcia Veldman of **Meadowlark Organic Farm** serves as market manager. She and husband Steve Cotter grow vegetables on a one-acre plot surrounded by rolling pasture and woodland; they grow all year with the help of a solar greenhouse. They sell at the Bloomington market and to Restaurant Tallent, a Bloomington eatery focused on Indiana cuisine. They are members of the Local

Growers' Guild, a group of growers, retailers, and citizens dedicated to southern Indiana food systems. The guild publishes an annual growers guide about where to buy local food and maintains a website listing CSA programs and farm internships.

» Like Rose Ridge in Ohio, **Stranger's Hill Organics** is another farm certified by the Ohio Ecological Food and Farm Association (OEFFA). "OEFFA is a reputable and longstanding organization, and we're proud to have been with them since the early days," says farm manager Vanessa Caruso. Only 6.5 miles from downtown Bloomington, Stranger's Hill has been growing organically since 1989 on land that has been under cultivation since 1816. Founders Dale and Lee Jones named the farm for their German shepherd, named Stranger, who held court at the top of a hill "as if he owned the place." In 2007 they acquired the nearby Howard Farm, an eighty-acre historic farm, by bringing in partners.

Dale Jones and Vanessa Caruso of Stranger's Hill Organics

As the farm manager, Caruso is responsible for almost everything "except dealing with the bank," she said. This includes ordering seed, negotiating equipment exchanges, coordinating the crew, tending stock, and working in the field. Caruso was born in the urban canyons of Manhattan, grew up in the fresh air of Kentucky, and came to Indiana University to pursue environmental studies. "I started with an interest in the ecological perspective, and while I worked at a community garden I became more interested in growing." She goes on to say how gardening and farming are completely different. "I need to choose more battles on the farm. I need to decide if I can be efficient enough, and that drives a lot of decisions." One example of choosing battles is preparing the soil for the winter. "In a garden we would cover the plot with cardboard and mulch and everything would be pristine to start in the spring. Because of the scale of the farm, it's not possible here."

In 2009 Stranger's Hill instituted a program to help underprivileged individuals in their community. CSA members have the option of chipping in for shares for distribution to low-income people or donating their shares when they go on vacation.

» Teresa Birtles of **Heartland Family Farm** has the bright-eyed energy one might expect from someone who grows custom crops for chefs, sells at the farmers' market, homeschools her children, maintains a one-hundred-member CSA, and has plans to help start a farm for an orphanage in Honduras.

Birtles offers countless heirloom vegetables, fruits, and herbs, as well as flowers grown by her daughter Sarah. Her main business is growing custom orders for chefs, including Dave Tallent of Tallent Restaurant and Jeff Finch of Finch's Brasserie, and market shoppers can benefit from her focus on flavor.

"I keep in mind what can be on the plate together, and that's what I grow. Then I look for varieties with the best flavor." Some of those companions on the plate might be Roma tomatoes, sweet onion, fennel and oregano, a combination perfect for an Italian-style salad or sauce. Birtles is best known for Italian tomato varieties like Florentino, Genovese, and the San Marzano, a paste tomato, as well as the Cherokee purple. She makes her own sauces and dried tomatoes through a small processor in the area. It is one thing to make a three-gallon batch of tomato sauce on the stove at home, but it is another undertaking altogether if your goal is a twenty-five-gallon steam kettle full of sauce. Adjusting the seasonings is a far greater challenge when working with such large quantities. "You can't just multiply a recipe and have it work out," Birtles says.

Teresa Birtles of Heartland Family Farm

Birtles practices intensive growing on the seven acres she has under cultivation. In the early season she plants salad greens, radishes, and green onions. Further along she replants with tomatoes, eggplant, cabbages, broccoli, cauliflower, and so on. In the fall she tills the ground, sows cover crops, and mulches with straw to enhance soil health. Chef Jeff Finch of Finch's Brasserie in Bloomington says that "going out to Teresa's Econoline van is like running out to the ice cream truck. There's always something delicious."

Indiana Summer Succotash

Jeff Lynch, Finch's Brasserie

Chef Jeff Finch takes advantage of his arrangement with Teresa Birtles of Heartland Family Farm to make a classic succotash with innovative ingredient combinations, switching vegetables as new ones come in season. Traditionally made with corn and lima beans, this edition showcases Romano beans—long, wide, flat Italian green beans. Finch prefers to cook each vegetable separately to preserve the individual flavors, then he warms everything together with the herbs right before serving.

¼ cup olive oil, divided

1 pound Romano beans or other green bean

1 cup sugar snap peas

1 cup fresh corn kernels (from about 1 ear)

½ cup diced sweet onion

¼ cup scallion

¼ cup diced sweet red bell pepper

1 tablespoon minced jalapeño pepper or other hot pepper

¼ cup white wine

1 tablespoon butter

Salt and pepper to taste

1 cup loosely packed chopped herbs, such as flat leaf parsley, chives, and purple basil

Preheat a skillet over medium-high heat. Add about a tablespoon of oil and the Romano beans. Season lightly with salt and pepper and sauté until bright and tender, about two minutes. Transfer to a plate. Repeat with sugar snap peas and corn kernels, then sauté onion, scallions and peppers together. Let vegetables cool.

When ready to serve, preheat skillet, add green beans, snap peas, corn, onions peppers, wine and butter. Toss together until warm; taste, and then season with salt and pepper. Toss in herbs right before serving.

» **Capriole Farmstead Goat Cheese** in Greenville, Indiana, is produced at a five-hundred-goat operation just over the state line from Louisville, Kentucky. The effervescent Judy Schad has created more than a dozen types of goat cheese, which she sells at farmers' markets as well as at retail. Her cheeses show up on restaurant cheese courses across the Midwest and beyond, and have won numerous awards from the American Cheese Society.

Many cheesemakers name their cheeses after the European cheese styles that inspire them. Not Schad. Hers have whimsical monikers that capture a sense of place: Wabash Cannonball, Blue River buttons, Old Kentucky Tomme, and Sophia, a luscious ripened cheese marbled with ash, named for her friend and distributor Sophia Solomon. O'Banon is an interpretation of the classic Banon, a pasteurized goat cheese, wrapped in chestnut leaves or grape leaves soaked in *eau de vie*. Capriole's kicked-up version uses Woodford Reserve Bourbon. The name is for Frank O'Bannon, the late Indiana governor. Julianna, an aged raw-milk cheese, is named for a Hungarian cheesemaking intern who loved to play around with the process and contributed to the creation of this new variation on the Old Kentucky.

When Judy and her husband, Larry Schad, relocated to the rolling hills of southern Indiana in 1976, they later discovered they had purchased his great-great-grandfather's farm, which dated to the 1870s. They had indeed returned home. Schad's closed herd of Nubian, Saanen, and Alpine goats benefit from the farmstead's priority on natural animal cycles. "We set them out to browse the woodlands as often as possible," said Schad. "Goats are smart animals and they know what's nutritious." Majestic Great Pyrenees dogs help guard the herd.

When Capriole launched commercially in 1988, goat cheese was nowhere near as popular as it is today. "It was not hard to beat the quality of what was coming in," she said. Even so, it was definitely a challenge to educate people to embrace new flavors. Schad says she thinks of cheese as "just like cooking, like making jelly or canning tomatoes or pears." Perhaps that focus on taste is one of the factors of her success.

》 Home to the National Maple Syrup Festival, **Burton's Maplewood Farm** in Medora, Indiana, produces two hundred gallons of pure maple syrup each season from its forest, which is no small feat, given that it takes about fifty to sixty gallons of sap to make a single gallon of syrup.

Operated by Patrick Burton and son Tim, the Burtons produce two hundred gallons of maple syrup annually. Despite being pretty far south in Indiana (about thirty miles or so from the Kentucky border), the Burtons remember their area as a former maple mecca. But the growing seasons have changed over the years, with a shorter maple season that starts earlier and does not last as long. But as long as the ground freezes in winter, the syrup business is safe.

Patrick and Tim Burton of Burton's Maplewood Farm

Maple syrup might be our continent's earliest sweetener. Native Americans taught settlers how to make it by tapping trees with stones and then using bark to funnel the sap into birch buckets. The sap was concentrated by dropping hot stones into the buckets. Today, the process is remarkably similar. At the first hint of spring, when the freeze/thaw cycles begin, sap comes up from the roots to nourish the branches. Trees are drilled, then plastic taps with tubes are "tapped" in with a hammer. The sap runs into a ten-gallon bucket, which is emptied into a larger bucket and then poured into a tank on the back of a truck. The truck is dispatched to the sugar shack, where the sap is pumped into a holding tank near the evaporator, a kind of giant rectangular saucepan with thermometers and indicators that ensure the sap never reaches a simmer. The sap, which tastes sweet but looks like water, is warmed until most of the liquid evaporates, leaving a rich, amber syrup. The syrup is then drawn off, filtered, graded, and bottled for market.

》 Matt and Mandy Corry produce meat, poultry, and eggs on **Schacht Farm** in Bloomington. After graduate school and starting careers—Matt in special education and Mandy in mental health and international adoption—the Corrys became more aware of how their food was produced. They decided to make a transition and set up business on a farm that had been in Mandy's family since the 1960s. They named it after an earlier farm family because they were moved by writings of Oscar Schacht, who emphasized doing the right thing versus the popular thing and raised animals naturally. Schacht's dairy farm was named Jersey Joy, and the former milk house is now where the Corrys live with their son Abe.

The Corrys consider themselves stewards of their animals and land, and they focus on heritage breeds and free-range feasting. They started in pork because they "wanted a good BLT." After buying one pig for their own consumption, they now keep dozens, and the pigs live in hog heaven, grazing on pasture where they dine on hickory nuts, walnuts, and wind-fallen apples. Their poultry enjoy bugs, grass, local grains, and organic kelp. Turkeys are the Bronze breed, which has been around since the 1700s and was recognized by the American Poultry Association in 1874.

» The sign for **McCullough's Fresh Homegrown Sweet Corn** occupies the entire side of the extra-large truck that Dan, Kaye, and Brandon McCullough use to haul their corn to market from Daviess County, Indiana. The line of market shoppers at the truck does not let up for hours. Dan McCullough says it is because the family has long nurtured a reputation for fresh, delicious corn. He plants several varieties of yellow, white, and bicolor sweet corn to cover the early, middle, and late seasons. Other producers also have pretty good corn, and you can even buy popcorn at the Bloomington market.

» Also at the Bloomington County Farmers' Market are Jim and Rebekah Fiedler of **Fiedler Family Farms**, third-generation producers of grass-fed and finished beef, pork, and lamb in Rome, Indiana. The family farm has been in operation since 1922.

Traders Point Creamery Farmers' Market

26 vendors

Saturdays, November through April; Fridays, May through October

9101 Moore Road, Zionsville

The Traders Point Green Market started as a winter market at the request of the farmers. They noticed that Traders Point had a heated barn that could serve as a perfect venue for operations like **Seven Springs Farm**, for instance, to sell its pastured chicken and eggs, and for **The Swiss Connection** to sell its farmstead cheese and pasture meat. With about a dozen winter vendors, including **Phelps Family Farm**, **Bluffwood Creek**, and **Grabow Orchard**, the scene was set to extend into the summertime. More than two dozen vendors sell everything from honey products to pet treats. See **Valentine Hill Farm** for whole grain breads and ready-to-top pizza crusts, **This Old Farm** for naturally fed chicken, lamb, beef, and pork, and **Redwine Family Farms** for all kids of vegetables, including heirloom tomatoes, beets, Swiss chard, and herbs. **Natural Born Juicers** will juice fruits and vegetables to order.

Before they launched the farmers' market on the outskirts of Indianapolis, physician Peter "Fritz" Kunz and his wife Jane Elder Kunz founded the Traders Point Creamery. Dr. Kunz is unusual in the medical field—doctors are notoriously focused on treating disease rather than enhancing health before any disease occurs. But Dr. Kunz is on a mission to change the way food is produced and advocates for a healthier diet based on whole foods. For that reason, you will not find skim or low-fat products from this dairy. Kunz says that skimming off the fat means it is no longer a "whole" food. That is a pretty dramatic business strategy, given our country's fear of fat. And Kunz believes dairy food should be produced from cows that eat grass, because grass infuses the milk with important nutrients and makes it superior to other feeds.

But there's more. Kunz also believes that a popular process, homogenization, disturbs the natural nutrients

Traderspoint Creamery in Zionsville

in the milk. The process, he says, prevents the natural separation of the fat molecules, impeding digestion. Thus, when you buy a half-gallon of Traders Point Creamery milk, the cream will be at the top, and you'll need to shake vigorously to reintegrate the cream into the milk. The creamery produces milk, raw-milk artisan cheese, and pourable yogurts, sold at farmers' markets as well as at the dairy.

In true visionary fashion, the Kunzes have created a dairy that serves as a food destination, with a weekly year-round farmers' market and a farm camp for schoolchildren in July and August. Thus, the facility is a well-oiled agri-tourism machine. Impressive buildings, all sturdy lumber structures, harken back to heritage architecture. A portable hen house is a spiffy dwelling to keep chickens whose job it is to process the cow pies. Visitors can tour the farm, either on their own or with a guide.

Each Friday shoppers wind their way through the countryside to reach Traders Point, just a few miles south of the village of Zionsville (which also operates a market on Saturday mornings). "It was the farmers who came up with the idea of a market here," says Kunz. "We had these big barns that were perfect for a winter market, and now we just continue all year round." Visitors to the Friday market can enjoy a farm menu outdoors during warm weather, or in the Loft Restaurant, a café that also offers frozen yogurt and homemade pies baked by the staff.

Jane Elder Kunz is a full partner in the operation and is the one who brings farming roots to the team. Her grandparents owned Cherry Basket Farm, still in operation in Omena, Michigan.

Broad Ripple Farmers' Market

Founded 1996

50+ vendors

Wednesdays, June
through September
Broad Ripple Indy
Park, 1550 Broad
Ripple Avenue,
Indianapolis

Saturdays, May
through November
Broad Ripple High
School, 1115 Broad
Ripple Avenue,
Indianapolis

The Broad Ripple Market boasts a lively mix of anything you would like to eat, including **My Dad's Sweet Corn**, which comes with a pledge that it was picked within the past twenty-four hours. **Seldom Seen Farm** is a first-generation vegetable farm growing in the clay loam of Hendricks County everything from radishes and red peppers to greens like kale and arugula to onions, scallions, and leeks. For meat, select from **Schacht Farm** and **Royer Farm**, as well as bison at **Circle L Bison Farm** or wild birds, goat, and rabbit at **Hilltop Farm**. **Yeager Farm Produce** is best known for melons and okra, as well as a generous variety of Asian vegetables, like bitter melon, Chu-Chu eggplant, and lemon cucumber. **Sunny Creek Farm** focuses on chemical-free production and also forages—one weekend they had thirty pounds of foraged elderberries. True to its name, the **American Persimmon Company** sells persimmons, and **Backyard Birds** makes edible products for wild birds; **Three Dog Bakery** sells dog treats. For an authentic crepe, stop by **3 Days in Paris** or get a baked delight from **Rene's Bakery**. **Willowfield Lavender Farm** is the spot for lavender products like soap and body butter.

Indianapolis City Market Farmers' Market

This market bills itself as the original farmers' market at the Indianapolis City Market. The renovated brick market building was constructed in 1886 and now is home to vendors selling artisan goods and ethnic foods, and the **Tomlinson Tap**, which features up to sixteen beers on tap at any given time. Indianapolis is the rare market with wineries—**Smith's Winery** and **Simmon's Winery and Farm Market** both have Indiana wine to sell. **Highland Angus Farm** sells beef. **VanAntwerp Farm** is known for stellar melons and tomatoes, and **Blitz Greenhouse** has gorgeous asparagus. **Local Folks Food** sells prepared foods, from blueberry jam to mushroom and vegetable pasta sauce.

Founded 1997

40 vendors

Wednesdays, May through October (outdoors); Wednesdays, November through April (inside City Market)

Market Street between Delaware and Alabama Streets, Indianapolis

Carmel Farmers' Market

About sixteen miles north of Indianapolis, the grand Palladium Center for Performing Arts reigns over the Carmel Farmers' Market. Each vendor has a sign indicating how many miles it travels to the Carmel market. **Mulberry Creek Herb Farm** travels 121 miles from Sandusky with herbs. Across the aisle, **Nading Farms** travels sixty-one miles with pork sausage, vegetables, fruits, and eggs; you can also find meat at **Phelps Family Farms** and **Homestead Heritage**. If you are looking for salad greens, visit **Good Life Farms**. For a nibble while you shop, stop by the **The Walking Waffle Company**, **Kuntry Side Bakery**, **Smokin' Hoosier BBQ**, or **Circle City Sweets**. Take home dessert from **Lisa's Pies** and a bottle to go with dinner at **Mallow Run Winery**.

Founded 1999

50+ vendors

Saturdays, May through October

Center Green, City Center Drive and Southwest Third Street, Carmel

Indiana's History of "Putting Up"

Canning, or "putting up" foods, is exploding almost as fast as farmers' markets as consumers embrace the idea of local food and strive to prolong the harvest by canning sauce, making pickles, and cooking up jams, jellies, and preserves. This American tradition has strong roots in Muncie, Indiana, longtime headquarters of the company that made Ball canning jars. Minnetrista is the forty-acre cultural center anchored by Oakhurst, the 1895 house of George Alexander Ball, which operates a weekly farmers' market. In 2009 it celebrated the 125th anniversary of the iconic Ball canning jar.

John L. Mason made it all possible when he patented the screw-top lid in 1858, opening a market for Ball. The Ball Brothers Glass Manufacturing Company moved to Muncie in 1887 after a fire devastated their Buffalo, New York, factory. The relocation was a strategic move that allowed the company to capitalize on the boom in midwestern natural gas, a component in glass production. Sand from the shores of Lake Michigan lent the blue and blue-green hue to jars. Today, only lids are manufactured in Muncie, but the local university stands as tribute to the area's glass jar heritage and the influence of the company's founders: Ball State University was funded by the Balls and donated to the state. Jarden Home Brands now owns the Ball brand and manufactures jars in Colorado.

The Ball Blue Book, the canner's bible, was introduced in 1909 and has been continually updated. After more than a century, it continues to be a go-to resource for canners.

And canning has caught on again. The company that produces the Ball brand mason jars reported that sales of canning equipment was up by 30 percent in 2009. Suburban canners are equal in number to rural canners, and half are under age forty. In 2011 Ball embarked on a program to host canning workshops at fifty farmers' markets across the country, and the company included donations to participating markets.

Shortcut Small-Batch Jam

Most recipes for jams and preserves call for bushels of fruit and pounds of sugar. If you have your own orchard, or even a few fruit trees, this approach makes sense. But some cooks want to experiment with flavor combinations, like blueberry basil jam, blueberry lime, strawberry rhubarb, and ginger rhubarb, to capture a variety of flavor from each fruit. For those folks, and for beginning canners, there is a better way, one that focuses on small batches.

Russ Parsons, who wrote *How to Pick a Peach: The Search for Flavor from Farm to Table,* published this shortcut method in the *Los Angeles Times*. He credits Sylvia Thompson, author of *The Kitchen Garden Cookbook,* for this elegantly simple way to make small-batch jam.

The technique: Cut up the fruit and weigh it. Add an equal weight of sugar. Bring it to a boil on top of the stove and then let it sit overnight to macerate. The next day, finish the jam, a couple of cups at a time, in a nonstick skillet. Cooked over medium-high heat, it will set in less than five minutes. That's all there is to it.

The jam has enough sugar to be processed in a water bath and stored in your pantry, although small batches are easy to store in the refrigerator or freezer.

Minnetrista Farmer's Market

Founded 2001

80+ vendors

Wednesdays, June through October; Saturdays, May through October; third Saturday of each month November through April

311 Joseph Street, Muncie

The farmers' market is a natural extension of the Ball estate. In the 1870s the matron of a nearby orphanage decided children needed to earn spending money. An orchard was planted, and children sold the fruit. Later, the Ball family bought the property, including the ten-acre orchard, now a focal point of Minnetrista activities. Find everything from eggs, popcorn, and **Sechler's** dill pickles in addition to vendors selling the bounty of Indiana fruit and vegetables. **Compulsion Coffee** keeps everyone caffeinated for shopping.

About Hoosier Pie

We have already met Paula Haney, whose Hoosier Mama Pie Company is based in Chicago. Her roots and inspiration are planted firmly in Indiana, where her mother grew up in a farm family of nine. It turns out she and her mother talked a lot about the pies that Hoosiers call their own.

During the growing season, fruit pies are filled with the season's bounty from the first strawberry to the last apple. But Haney's true talent comes in presenting the story of "desperation pies," those pies of winter put on the table when the apple barrel is empty and berries a distant memory. These are the sugar cream and vinegar pies, the ones made with pantry staples and not much else.

The traditional Hoosier pie fillings have only three ingredients: cream, flour, and sugar. Haney tells about how easy it was for farm wives to make a pie. "You could pour the dry ingredients into the pie shell, then top it off with cream and stir it with your finger. You didn't even have to wash any dishes." Perhaps that's the origin of the expression "easy as pie." One staple you will not find in a traditional desperation pie: eggs.

"My mother told me eggs were a luxury because that was what people sold," says Haney. "But often they'd have some sugar and some cream from a cow. And some people had stills, so they'd add a little distilled rose water, or a little ground nutmeg."

Haney made a hobby of buying up vintage cookbooks and saw a recipe for sugar cream pie from 1816, the year Indiana became a state. A 1965 Farm Journal *Complete Pies* cookbook praises pioneer pie bakers for ingenuity but discourage readers from making their own desperation pies. Haney defied that recommendation, and now her desperation pies are some of her most popular offerings.

Clark County Farmers' Market

The Clark County Market at Jeffersonville features Tim Sells, who is known for tomatoes; Mary Graf, and David and Gail Crum, who sell produce; and Jackie Fouts who sells luscious strawberries. The Miller family serves up baked goods.

Founded 1987

7 vendors

Tuesdays and Saturdays, May through October

Chestnut and Locus Streets, Jeffersonville

Refugees Find Welcoming Connections at the Farm

Although many farmers are working land passed down over generations, there is another category of farmers not only working for a living but also striving for a connection to their homeland and former way of life.

Farming is all about connection—to the land, to our history, to family. Imagine having to flee your home country, one steeped in rural traditions of farming and weaving, and finding yourself in a city, entirely foreign, filled with concrete and fast vehicles and people speaking a language you do not understand.

Maria Figueroa noticed the plight of some such refugees in Indianapolis, and set out to find a way to make them feel welcome and connected. She phoned me on a rainy afternoon to tell me about her work with the Karen (pronounced kah-REN), a group who fled persecution by a military dictatorship in Burma. "I wanted to help them find healing and identity," she says. "My hope is that they will find integration and eventually a business."

The healing and identity comes from the Karen's deep farming roots in their native land. Figueroa's solution is elegantly simple: through old-fashioned telephone networking, she found Carol Waterman and her husband Bruce of Waterman Farm, who offered up two of their fifty acres for the Karen, at no charge, just to help—and it was enough for a start. The Watermans have what is called a Hoosier Homestead Farm, one that has been in the same family for more than one hundred years. They operate a farm market on their farm from strawberry season in May through pumpkin time in October, as well as at another location during peak production.

Figueroa's matchmaking goes beyond the two acres at the Waterman Farm. She has recruited churches to donate use of acreage in exchange for donations of fresh food to food banks and also founded the Refugee Resource and Research Institute to address the issue in a more formal capacity.

Historic Lafayette Farmers' Market

Founded 1839

40+ vendors

Tuesday and Saturdays, May through October

Fifth Street between Main and Columbia Streets, Lafayette

Historic downtown Lafayette is the place to be Saturday mornings. Start with a caffeine fix at **Greyhouse Coffee and Supply Company** or **K. Dees Coffee**, then set out to score vegetables from **LongHouse Farm**, **Markle Farm & Greenhouses**, **Raney Farms**, **Pleasant Acre Farm**, **Carroll County Crops**, and **Kelly's Flowers & Vegetables**. Pick up fruit from **Butera Family Orchard**, beef, pork, and lamb from **Cleaver Family Farms**, and poultry and eggs from **Thistle Byre Farm** and **Tranquil Ridge Farms**. **Cattle Dog Bakery** brings the pup treats. **Wabash & Riley Honey Company** goes beyond honey to offer preserves and produce. Once you have filled your canvas bags and enjoyed a baked treat from **Klein Brot Haus Bakery & Restaurant**, stroll a block to take in the Tippecanoe County Courthouse.

South Bend Farmers' Market

The South Bend Market harkens back to 1911 and was incorporated in its current location in 1924. The current market building dates to 1972, constructed in the shape of an H, which allows vendors to back up to their stall doors. It is punctuated by a restaurant in the center, serving breakfast and lunch. Pick up your five-a-day vegetable servings by choosing from **Maple Land Farms**, **The Glenn Vite Farm**, **Wolf Farms & Greenhouses**, **Johnson's Produce**, and **Hetler Farms**. Buy fruit from **Hillside Orchard**, **Klug Family Farms**, and **Walt Skibbe Farms**, whose grandparents sold at the market in the 1920s. Find chicken at **Hiatt's Poultry** and beef at **Sawyer's Meats**. The South Bend Market is a baked goods bonanza with a dozen vendors to choose from, including **Parcell's Pantry**, **The Baker's Dozen**, and **Kris' Kountry Kitchen**.

Founded 1911

100+ vendors

Tuesdays, Thursdays, and Saturdays, all year; first Fridays, May through September

1105 Northside Boulevard, South Bend

Illinois

In the 1970s, federal farm policy encouraged farmers to consolidate their crops and focus on commodities. Illinois farmers tell me that at that time, the United States Department of Agriculture decided the fertile soil of Illinois was best suited for corn and soybeans. In an ironic step, a state with great soil and ample water stopped producing food for people to eat and focused on commodity crops used primarily for manufacturing or for animal feed. But a few stubborn holdouts and some relative newcomers have created a portfolio of farms well suited to a robust farmers' market scene, making Illinois an excellent place to discuss farmland preservation.

Market at the Square

Founded 1979

160 vendors

Saturdays, May through
November

Illinois and Vine Streets,
Urbana

*Lisa Bralts, manager
for Urbana's Market at
the Square*

Market manager Lisa Bralts sees to it that all the products sold at the Market at the Square come from Illinois, which is not without its challenges. Some Indiana farms may be close geographically, but the Illinois-only focus works for the market. She also sees that the Urbana market connects with its shoppers in the high-tech arena of social media. She tweets on Twitter, posts photos on Flickr, and maintains a blog with news on the best seasonal produce, along with links to farm websites. The market's active Facebook page has around three thousand "friends," and Bralts posts weekly videos about what is fresh that week. She is also a contributor to the local public radio station, all with an eye on boosting traffic and enthusiasm for the farmers' market.

Tall, willowy, and blonde, Bralts is the perfect illustration of wholesome good health that comes from farm-fresh food. She is at ease with prickly personalities who want to sell things not found on any farm, and quick to respond to information requests. Market vendors have called her brilliant. Bralts is an employee at the City of Urbana, which operates the market, and also serves as an economic development officer for the city. On market days her work begins at 5 A.M. With her badge around her neck and site plan in hand, she deploys the troops to make sure tents are set up, the welcoming sandwich-board sign in place, and everything ready when the market opens promptly at 7 A.M. She makes the rounds with a clicker to count shoppers, fields questions from vendors and patrons, then sees that are tents taken down again and everything swept and tidy by two o'clock.

A Day in the Life of a Market Manager

A farmers' market is a performance, like a symphony, carefully rehearsed. But then it turns into a jazz combo, filled with improvisation. It begins with a dark empty stage, then a few people begin to set up and early birds trickle in. Suddenly begins the crescendo of crowds and activity, then dwindling, then quiet again. Here we learn about a day in the life of a farmers' market in the words of Lisa Bralts, market director, Urbana's Market at the Square.

4:30 A.M.: **Wake up**. I'm completely terrified of missing my alarm on Saturday mornings, so I set three of them—4:30, 4:45, and 5:00 A.M.. I'm always up by 4:30, though, and I'm usually at my office at City Hall by 5:00 A.M.

5:00–5:30 A.M.: **Load the pickup.** While our market site is in the parking lot right across the street, all of our informational materials— EBT/credit/debit stuff, merchandise, water coolers, etc.—need to be hauled over in the pickup known as "Truckie." I also check messages and email to see if there are any last-minute cancellations.

5:30 A.M.: **Two market staff members arrive.** One is our groundskeeper, who takes another pickup to our offsite storage (about a mile away) to haul over our tents, tables, chairs, trash barrels, and traffic barricades. The other is my assistant, who does everything I do onsite and works with me after we close. Occasionally, my assistant gets a day off, so I have a paid market staffer come in at 6:00 to help out during market hours (7 A.M.–noon). I haven't had a Saturday off in three seasons (eighty-three markets). Fortunately, I don't work Mondays during the season.

5:35 A.M.: **Go to Starbucks.** This whole thing would not be possible without strong coffee.

5:45 A.M.: **Arrive at market site.** My assistant and I unload the truck, and then we unlock our electrical receptacles and bring recycling bins from city hall, which is right across the street.

5:45–7:00 A.M.: **Assist vendors.** Directing new and weekly vendors to their spaces begins almost immediately and continues for the next hour. During this time, we are also setting up our tents and tables—our regular ones and also any for special events we might be hosting—filling water coolers, arranging our printed matter/signs/merchandise, and getting the credit card machine/market tokens ready. My assistant and I both walk the market a few times to make sure everyone is in the right space and to see if anyone has questions or needs something. Someone usually does.

7:00 A.M.: **Market officially begins!** Our groundskeeper puts up all the barricades to prevent vehicles from entering the market. By now, patrons are coming in, and many of them want to avail themselves of our market's token system, which allows them to use their credit, debit, or LINK card at the market. We're also starting to direct community groups, whose area is on the north end of the market, to their spaces, which we do until 8:00 A.M. The groundskeeper then leaves until 11:30 A.M.

7 A.M.noon: **Market tasks.** It doesn't stop after we get set up. Shortly after 7:00, my assistant hands out the vendor envelopes, which contain paperwork and checks from the previous week's SNAP token redemption. All morning long, we are answering patron questions, helping them find vendors, running credit/debit/LINK transactions, selling T-shirts and tote bags, handing out receipts to vendors and community groups for their booth payments, processing payments for booth space for the next week, counting patrons, and walking the market to ensure things are running smoothly. I also take photos every Saturday.

Noon–12:30 P.M.: **Market closes.** We tear down our tent and tables, lock electrical receptacles, and accept tokens from vendors. We count the tokens with them and fill out paperwork, so it takes a little time. The groundskeeper removes the barricades to allow vehicles into the market and takes down all our other tents, tables, chairs, etc., hauling them back to offsite storage. During peak season, we work with the Foodbank to get excess grower produce donated, which is happening after noon.

12:30–1:30 P.M.: **Market reconciliation.** This task was new in 2010 with the introduction of our credit/debit/LINK system. My assistant and I haul everything back into my building, and then count redeemed tokens, matching them up with each vendor's paperwork. We also count the tokens we didn't distribute to patrons. We run the batch report from the credit/debit/LINK machine and match up all our receipts as well. This can take up to an hour, but when we're done, my assistant is done. The groundskeeper usually comes back at 1:30 after taking everything back to storage. They sign their payroll sheets and leave.

1:30–2:00 P.M.: **Putting the market to bed. Mostly.** This is when I enter all reconciliation numbers into a spreadsheet, created for me by the city's finance department, and send it off to them for vendor checks. I check the day's notes, look at the attendance sheet and map to see how things played out, and write myself a few notes before leaving. There are still a few things I'll have to take care of on Tuesday, but I can only work until two o'clock on Market days.

Farmers at Urbana's Market at the Square

» The Market at the Square is set up with aisles, with longest-term vendors getting prime spots at the entrance. But even though **Prairie Fruits Farm** is toward the center of the market, there is no lack of buyers. Owners Leslie Cooperband and husband Wes Jarrell started making delicious, fresh goat cheese while also serving on the faculty of the University of Illinois College of Agriculture, Consumer and Environmental Sciences. They met while they were both soil experts at the University of Wisconsin–Madison, and Jarrell's opportunity to move to the University of Illinois gave them the chance to acquire acreage . . . and four goats. Now the first certified farmstead in Illinois, Prairie Fruits is home to a herd of La Mancha and Nubian goats, including eighty milking does.

Leslie Cooperband of Prairie Fruits Farm

Even though the affordability of acreage made her creamery possible, Cooperband refers to central Illinois as a dairy desert. Hers is the first licensed farmstead cheesemaking facility in Illinois, and being the only one means she does not have the strong network that dairies in Wisconsin enjoy.

During kidding season in the spring, Cooperband and Jarrell invite friends of the farm to a "baby shower" to meet the new goats. Cooperband makes bloomy rind cheeses with charming names like Little Bloom on the Prairie and Angel Food. Sometimes the Angel Food gets wrapped in a sycamore leaf from the farm, soaked in Illinois Chambourcin wine, and christened Prairie Blazing Star Banon. And as if her expanding selection of cheeses were not enough, Cooperband traveled with Jarell to Italy to study gelato making with an eye toward adding ice cream to their offerings.

Prairie Fruits Farm experienced a firsthand example of development bumping into farmland preservation—a new road will soon run right through their alfalfa field and affect two other farms that date to the Civil War. Various Champaign-Urbana agencies wanted to capture stimulus funding provided by the Obama administration to complete a ring road that had been on and off the books for more than thirty years. Farmland preservationists deemed the project ill advised because growth was stalled due to economic decline, and so they declared it a road to nowhere because the cash-strapped city and state cannot afford to install concomitant infrastructure like access roads, electricity, and sewers. And yet officials went ahead after a long, hard fight, and the road will be built, having a direct effect on exactly the kinds of farms that the country needs to diversify its food production.

» Stan Scott Schutte has produced organic meat at **Triple S Farms** in Stewardson, Illinois, since about 1980. His slogan, "We Grow Taste," speaks to his devotion to healthy soil. He raises Red Angus cows on certified organic pasture, as well as Tamworth Berkshire pigs, Broad Breasted Bronze turkeys, and Cornish Cross chickens. Schutte farms with his son Ryan, daughter Kristen, and a few other staffers. Three dogs and a couple dozen cats round out the farmworkers.

In 2006 Schutte received the organic farmer of the year award from MOSES, the Midwest Organic and Sustainable Education Service, for practicing outstanding land stewardship, innovation, and outreach. The chickens are free range and produced without genetically modified grains. A lifelong farmer, Schutte went into organics in response to the hog market crash in 1997. "I wasn't making money and had to do something different," he says, adding that he gets a little impatient with his conventional farmer colleagues. "They plant corn and soybeans and don't try anything else, then complain when their businesses don't do well."

Schutte began producing heritage pigs because he knew how to raise pork, and then he added other animals. He continues to offer new products, including what he calls cottage bacon, a cured pork shoulder for people who like bacon but want less fat. He has also started meat clubs. He considers his business model proprietary, but he hints that his clubs are similar to a CSA model, where people pay for shares and then pick up their allocation throughout the season. "We had maximized our sales at the market, but now [our presence there] is a great way to introduce people to the meat club. People like having first dibs on our meat," he said.

Schutte sums up the future of farming with a philosophy that is gaining traction: "For years I've been telling people that they need a farmer. Just like they have a doctor, a dentist, and a lawyer, they need a professional to feed them." Schutte has a particularly close relationship with his eaters: every year he hosts a customer-appreciation party at his farm. Recently, more than two hundred patrons showed up for tasting and touring.

» Ruzica "Seka" Cuk and her **Pekara Bakery** in Champaign, Illinois, represent another story of the American dream made real. A native of Serbia, she was an exchange student in Mt. Zion in the 1970s. She was visiting her host family with her husband and daughter in 1992 when the Bosnian War was flaring up. They initially planned to stay only for the summer to escape the unrest.

"While we were visiting, the war reached a crisis, and we didn't go back," she says. "We had a new home and only two suitcases." Cuk's host family helped shepherd the immigration process, and when her daughter was out of high school, Cuk decided to open her own business.

Dusan Katic of Pekara Bakery plans to open his own bakery.

"I had a hard time finding good bread, so I wanted a bakery. And I wanted it in downtown Champaign because downtown reminds me of home," she says. When fellow Serb Dusan Katic strolled in looking for a job, he brought a love of science to the business; he is now head baker. Pekara sells thirteen kinds of bread in addition to other pastries and coffee cakes, and they have a booming business selling to restaurants as well. Cuk credits the farmers' market with helping grow her business. "We have many more Urbana people coming to find us," she said.

Katic is currently scouting places in Peoria for his own bakery, where he hopes to have a hand in transforming our culture to one that is closer to the one he first tasted in the French Foreign Legion and learned through the influence of his parents, Serbian immigrants like Cuk. "I saw how people relate to food," he says, and each other, for that matter. "People sit down to eat together. They don't eat on the run."

He says we have lost the face of our food, "the human part" of our food, as he calls it, and replaced it with "cold aisles of sliced bread." He says, "People want sliced bread to eat in the car and throw the crusts out the window," claiming to have witnessed crusts of bread flying out the window of a pick-up truck. This metaphor for how we have lost our connection as eaters is what drives Katic to search the countryside for the right place to make a difference, to set up a bakery to make artisan bread. "We're waging war against mediocrity," he says. "In France, there's a bakery for every fifteen hundred people. In Peoria, there's only one" artisan bakery. According to Katic, the metropolitan area of Peoria, at more than 370,000, is 245 bakeries short. In time, with the opening of Katic Breads, he will bring that number down to 244. His future wife, Carissa Graham, will make the sweet pastries.

Serendipitously, Katic and Graham met at the Urbana at the Square Market. "She was asking me about the bread and I said 'nice dress,' and I ran into her at the market again a few weeks later, and a year later we were engaged." Obviously they had more in common than an interest in fashion.

» Also selling baked goods at the market is the **Red Oak Comfort Food & Pie Company** from historic Bishop Hill, Illinois, a village established by Swedish immigrants in 1846, now a National Landmark Village on the National Registry of Historic Places.

Bob Kleiss of **Kleiss Produce Farm** wanted to grow "the corn no one else has." His wagonload of Illini X-tra Sweet corn draws a big crowd. The variety was developed at the University of Illinois at Urbana-Champaign more than fifty years ago and sold by the company Illinois Foundation Seeds for farm stands and home gardeners.

Kim Campbell of Campbell Apiaries

The **Moore Family Farm** has sold meat and poultry, vegetables, and stone-milled flours at the market for more than twenty years and thus has the prime spot at the market. There are also breads from **Homestead Bakery** and **Stewart's Artisan Breads**, and honey from **Campbell Apiaries**.

The market also welcomes artisans like Jill Miller of **Hooey Batiks**, who creates wearable batik art with food and nature motifs as well as other clever whimsical designs; hand-carved and painted gourds from **Michelle Faires**; and **Jeff Jones Photography**, whose photographs include a series of barns from the area. The artisans and food vendors are intermingled.

Just steps away from the Urbana market is **Common Ground Co-op**, an intimate grocery store that sells a lot of the same produce, but all week long.

Leslie Cooperband's Goat Cheese Ice Cream

This recipe calls for 12 egg yolks. Use the 12 whites for an angel food cake to accompany the ice cream; egg whites also freeze well for future use.

MAKES ABOUT FIVE CUPS

1 quart half-and-half

1 cup sugar

12 egg yolks

½ cup fresh goat cheese (8 ounces)

Combine half-and-half and sugar in a large saucepan over medium heat, stirring to dissolve sugar. Heat to a simmer, when bubbles form around the edge. Meanwhile, whisk the egg yolks in a large bowl. Slowly pour one cup of the warm milk into the yolks, whisking constantly. Slowly stir yolks back into the cream mixture, mixing well.

Cook over medium heat, stirring constantly, just until the mixture thickens to coat the back of a spoon, or reaches 185 degrees, about 6 minutes. Do not boil. Strain through a fine strainer into a clean bowl. Stir in the goat cheese until melted. Cover and refrigerate until thoroughly chilled, at least 3 hours. Freeze in an ice cream machine according to the manufacturer's directions.

Territory Farmers' Market

Founded 2004

20 vendors

Sundays, May through October

Owners Club, 2000 Territory Drive, Galena

Lovely Galena, in the top corner of Illinois near the Mississippi River, draws farmers from Illinois, Iowa, and Wisconsin. Here you will find **Life is Good Beef**, **Kristi's Perfect Produce**, **Trusted Earth Farm and Forage**, **Barb's Garden and Pantry**, and **Arnold Farm**. Get some pickles from **Gramp's Gourmet Foods**, or a sweet-delicious snack from **Jo Daviess Gold Kettle Corn**.

America Loses an Acre of Farmland Every Minute

In my travels across the Midwest I spotted bumper stickers and canvas bags emblazoned with "No farms, No food." This reminder comes to us from the people behind American Farmland Trust, and the alarm bell is increasingly important as so much rich farmland falls to development. From 1982 to 2007, the eight midwestern states covered in this book lost 4.4 million acres of farmland to subdivisions, roads, and other development. The loss is staggering—that 4.4 million acres translates into almost seven thousand square miles, an area slightly smaller than New Jersey, just in these eight states alone. It is land that we will not get back.

Enter American Farmland Trust, the nonprofit launched in 1980 by a group of farmers and conservationists for the sole purpose of stemming the loss of farmland. They credit their efforts with saving three million acres of farmland to date. In a large country that was settled largely by practically giving lands to its citizens, we have been trained to believe that there is plenty more, and there will always be a place to grow food.

American Farmland Trust is the only national organization focused on land availability. By protecting our land base, we are tied to revitalizing rural communities and also to food security and the environment. If we look back again to the Homestead Acts where people bought land at a reasonable price by committing to farm, we remember that people grew food to feed themselves *and* to trade. As towns grew up, they became places to gather, worship, go to school, and buy goods at the general store. Some of these towns became great cities, and they sprawled onto the farmland that drew people to this region in the first place.

Right now there is no permanent policy that protects farmland. There are state-funded initiatives to buy land easements, meaning the state buys the development rights to the property to protect it and keep it in agriculture. The farmer still owns the property and can still farm, but development rights are permanently removed, thus keeping the land in agriculture. Such initiatives protect the land from becoming a future shopping center or subdivision.

The urban edge, meaning the borders of cities, is where farmland is most vulnerable. The collapse of the housing bubble in 2008 and increasing fuel costs make a one-hour commute even more financially difficult for those who live farther away from urban centers. Thus, some sprawl may be contained in the immediate future. But if support for protection programs disappears at the urban edge, so will agriculture. And these are the areas where ten-acre plots or other smaller, farmers'-market-friendly farms can be set up with easy access to the city markets. That said, the economic downturn that began in 2008 did have a few high points in the bleakness. A few Illinois farmers bought back land they had sold to developers five years before.

The Land Connection Rescues At-Risk Acreage

About ninety-five miles northwest of Urbana, almost to Peoria, is Congerville, home to the Brockman's central Illinois farming dynasty.

Terra, the eldest, founded The Land Connection, a nonprofit that rescues farmland and trains novice farmers. Teresa Santiago, another Brockman sister, grows organic fruit and herbs. Henry, the youngest, owns the legendary Henry's Farm and is the rock star of the Evanston Farmers' Market just north of Chicago.

Terra Brockman's farm-saving venture started simply enough. After living in New York City and Japan, she returned to visit her family and noticed an alarming number of subdivisions cropping up on the region's rich farmland. She tells us that Illinois has been losing one hundred thousand acres of farmland per year since 1995 (1.5 million acres as of 2010). Of the remaining farmland, 70 percent is used to grow commodity corn, a crop highly dependent on chemicals, which does not feed people in Illinois and does not pay farmers an adequate income without government subsidies. "This model is not sustainable," she says.

Brockman founded The Land Connection on a simple premise: buy farmland that is at risk and use it to train novice farmers in sustainable and organic methods. The farmland stays in agriculture, and people can try out farming and get some training before they make the big commitment of buying their own land. During Land Connection tours, visitors can learn about raising shaggy highland cattle, which grow remarkably well in the Midwest because they are accustomed to a chilly climate, and about using portable chicken coops to allow for poultry to enjoy a nourishing bug diet as they peck over the fields of harvested grain, leaving it fertilized before moving on—and their coop moves with them.

Aside from training new farmers, Brockman's organization created the Midwest Farm Connection, a sort of matchmaking service to help people find a farm. Such a service is ideal for connecting new farmers with those who want to retire but may not have a family member to continue the farming tradition. The Land Connection also has an agriculture easement model to help farmers who are interested in preserving the farming tradition on their property.

Although her demeanor is calm and understated, it is clear that Brockman feels a fire to accomplish her goal of advancing chemical-free farming in an area that is anything but.

Downtown Evanston Farmers' Market

Founded 1975

35+ vendors

Saturdays, May through November

University Place and Oak Avenue, Evanston

Roy Elko of **Elko's Produce and Greenhouse** has been selling in Evanston since its inaugural year. **Heartland Meats** raises Piedmontese beef, an Italian breed known for lean meat and tender texture. Get gorgeous tomatoes and other vegetables from **Lake Breeze Organics**, and be sure to enjoy a scone from **Bennison's Bakery**. **The Talking Farm** advocates for urban farming and sells seedlings. We met some of the Evanston vendors in other chapters—**Seedling Fruit**, **Traders Point Creamery**, and **Nichols Farm and Orchard**.

Henry's Farm

» Perhaps Evanston's most famous farmer is Henry Brockman, who grows more than 630 varieties of vegetables on his farm nestled in the fertile Mackinaw River Valley not far from Congerville, Illinois, about 160 miles from the Evanston market. He has been a fixture there since 1993 and claims to feed two hundred families from his five acres in central Illinois by selling at the Evanston Market and through his CSA. His eggs sell out before the market even opens because people show up in pajamas before dawn to make sure they don't miss out.

Brockman embraces what you could call the "so what" philosophy of farming. He explained it to a group touring his farm: "If my beans fail, so what?" he said. "I have other things to sell. If my corn fails, so what? I have 629 other crops." Indeed, a visit to Brockman's tent at the Evanston market is a head-spinning celebration of the senses. Wooden crates (no plastic here) are stacked with every imaginable variety of green and bean, plus a variety of beets to make a gorgeous bouquet.

This philosophy illustrates the benefit of diversity, which is that a farmer does not have all his agriculture eggs in one basket. If a commodity farmer growing corn and soybeans has a crop failure, the entire season is jeopardized. If Brockman has a failure, he can make up the difference with other vegetables. And if you think that a five-acre vegetable farm would only offer a subsistence living, think again. Brockman grosses more than $100,000 for his effort. Granted, it's hot, sticky, cold, rainy, up-before-dawn effort, but nonetheless he shows that it can be done.

Brockman is also famous for another effort, which made the front page of the *Chicago Tribune*: he charges for plastic bags, the ubiquitous fixture of markets everywhere, and a big source of litter along rural highways. While he is sure to dismiss his designation as a rock star, a stop by his stand reveals a small congregation, discussing the vegetables, lingering as if cherishing their backstage pass.

Henry Brockman of Henry's Farm is known for his commitment to organic growing

» Beth Sakaguchi Eccles of **Green Acres** also sells at the Evanston Market. She comes from a farming tradition that dates back two generations when her grandfather emigrated from Japan and started a truck farm in northwest Indiana in the 1930s. Beth never intended to embrace farm life but was drawn back in: after studying business at Purdue University and later working at the university and getting married, the Eccleses grew greenhouse vegetables for their family table. When they had a surplus, they started considering the idea of selling at a farmers' market.

"I like living on the farm and smaller town life," says Eccles. "But I need to be around a lot of people. I like to bring my daughter to show her the diversity of people in the city. My dad and grandfather focused on growing the vegetables, but I need some interaction."

Now Beth and husband Brent grow vegetables, with an emphasis on Asian varieties, and sell at the Green City (Chicago) and Evanston markets. The distinctive vegetables are certainly a draw, like Japanese eggplants of all shapes and Japanese sweet potatoes with almost crimson skin and pale gold flesh.

Incidentally, the Green Acres name came decades before the TV show from the late 1960s, starring Eddie Albert as a successful businessman following his dream of becoming a farmer, and his socialite wife, played by Eva Gabor, who adored "a penthouse view" definitely not found on their farm. People will occasionally come up to Eccles's station and sing the TV theme song for her.

Beth introduced me to Asian sweet potatoes. The tagine recipe on page 131—essentially a vegetable stew—was inspired by Chef Jason Hammel, who has had it on the menu at Lula Café in Chicago for as long as I can remember. My own version riffs on his after he told me how to make it while we were socializing in front of the Green Acres table. He serves it over couscous, and I find it is equally good cold for a leftover lunch.

Beth Eccles is a third-generation farmer

Sweet Potato Chickpea Tagine

SERVES SIX AS A MAIN COURSE

2 tablespoons olive oil

2 medium onions, diced

1 teaspoon coriander seed

1 teaspoon cumin seed

1 teaspoon turmeric

1 teaspoon salt

½ teaspoon cayenne pepper

2 tablespoons minced fresh ginger

3 cloves garlic, minced

2 pounds sweet potatoes (about three),
peeled and cut into ½-inch pieces

2 cups cooked chickpeas (garbanzo beans)

½ cup raisins

1 28-ounce can crushed tomatoes

1 cup vegetable stock

½ cup cilantro leaves, minced

Preheat a large skillet or sauté pan over medium-high heat. Add oil and onions; cook, stirring occasionally, until tender and golden, about 8 minutes. Meanwhile, crush coriander and cumin in a mortar and pestle or with the bottom of a heavy pan, then stir together with turmeric, salt, and cayenne pepper. Add ginger and garlic to the onions, then stir in the spices and cook another 3-5 minutes to let the spices color the onions, stirring to prevent garlic from burning.

Add sweet potatoes, chickpeas, raisins, tomatoes, and vegetable stock and simmer about 20 minutes or until potatoes are fork-tender. Stir in cilantro.

Woodstock Farmers' Market

Founded 1992

40+ vendors

Tuesdays and Saturdays, June through September

Woodstock Square, near Cass and Clay Streets

Woodstock is a producer-only market surrounding the historic Woodstock Square, where musicians perform in the gazebo. Vendors include **Prairie Pure Cheese**, **May's Honey Farm**, **Windy Ridge Acres**, **Providence Farms**, and **Frog Alley Farms**. For fruit, stop at **Royal Oak Orchard** and **Paul Friday Farms**. Get a treat from **Tarts and Truffles**, **Ethereal Confections**, **Jaci's Cookies**, or **Tasty Bites and Treats**.

Peoria Riverfront Market

18 vendors

Saturdays, May through October

300 Water Street, Peoria

This market has a broad array of vegetables and fruits from **Hartz Produce**, **L&L Produce**, and **Jenkins Farm Market**. **White Chimney Farm** specializes in heirloom varieties. **Plow Creek Farm** features raspberries, blackberries, blueberries, and strawberries. **Greengold Acres** has free-range eggs and chickens, grass-fed beef, and organic fruit—be sure to pick up one of their pies. **Organic Pastures** also has high-quality meat and poultry. Grab something sweet from the **Cookie Shack** or **Braker's Dozen**, and pick up a loaf from the **Peoria Bread Company**.

The Old Capitol Farmers' Market

Shopping at the farmers' market at the Old Capitol in Springfield is an experience steeped in history. Abraham Lincoln's law office is just across the way, and his presidential library and museum are within walking distance. The Old Capitol itself is open to the public, and visitors can see where Lincoln argued cases during his decades-long career as a lawyer before becoming president.

The market has more than fifty vendors, including vegetable purveyors **Rothenbach Farms**, **Veenstra's Vegetables**, **Heck's Harvest**, and **Odelehr Farms**. For fruit, look for **Fortschneider's Orchard**, **Berry Best Farm**, and **Apple Hill of Scott County**. Meat lovers have a bonanza here with **Tripe S Farms**, **Bear Creek Farm & Ranch**, **Knob Hill Livestock Company**, **Tallgrass Prairie Farms**, and **Scovill Creek Farm**. **Vanderpool Apiary** is your source for honey. **Afterthought Farm** raises Alpine dairy goats for milk, cheese, and lotions.

Chef Michael Higgins of the 125-year-old restaurant Maldaner's hosts weekly demos at the Saturday market, after scouting it out on Wednesday to get a sense for what will be plentiful. "Farmers say to me 'you must have cooked with *this* today' because this is what everyone's buying." Higgins is a native of the San Francisco Bay area, a place noted for small farms and local food. He is another example of how chefs can lead the charge in introducing people to fresh, local foods.

"In the Bay area, we could always get fava beans," says Higgins. "I couldn't find them here in 1984, and I couldn't find anyone to grow them. I convinced Suttil's [Farm in Springfield] to grow some by offering to buy the seed. Now everyone grows them." Higgins adds that sometimes people just need a gentle prod: farmers sometimes just want to know they will make money on a venture.

Founded 2000

50+ vendors

Wednesdays and Saturdays, May through October

Adams Street between Fifth and Second Streets, Springfield

Roasted Pumpkin, Baby Greens, and Watercress Salad

Michael Higgins, Maldaner's

While sometimes the seasons sneak up and surprise us, there is one unmistakable moment when summer transitions into fall: when the hard-shell squash varieties arrive: pumpkins, butternut, acorn, turban squash. The multi-golden hues send us into the kitchen. Higgins shares an innovative way to spice up pumpkin.

Pumpkin

3 cups diced cooking pumpkin, such as Fairy Tale or Banana, or butternut squash

¼ cup olive oil

2 tablespoons chili spice blend

Salt and pepper to taste

Salad Greens with Apple Cider Vinaigrette

4 cups baby greens

2 bunches watercress, cleaned and stemmed

6 tablespoons grape seed oil or other light-tasting oil

2 tablespoons apple cider vinegar

¼ teaspoon Dijon-style mustard

Preheat oven to 400 degrees and position rack in the center. Whisk together olive oil and spice blend and toss with pumpkin. Place on a baking sheet and roast until barely fork tender but not too soft, about ten to fifteen minutes. Let cool to room temperature.

Clean greens and watercress. Dry and toss together. Store covered in the refrigerator until ready to serve. In a small bowl, whisk together oil, vinegar, and mustard until thoroughly emulsified. To serve, divide pumpkin between serving plates and top with greens, making sure that the pumpkin shows underneath the greens. Drizzle with dressing and serve.

Heritage Turkeys Come Home to Roost

The turkey is an authentically American bird, indigenous to both North America and South America. But something went terribly wrong from that time when the turkey was venerated as part of our culture to today, given the birds found in supermarkets every November. The breed found in grocery stores since the 1960s is called the Broad-Breasted White, now overbred to have a larger breast volume, to the point where the turkeys are so top heavy they cannot stand up properly.

People are taking a new look at the centerpiece of the table and are choosing a heritage turkey. These turkeys are direct descendants from the first domesticated flocks—breeds with names like Narragansett, White Midget, and Jersey Buff—that until a few years ago teetered on the brink of extinction. Now, not only are the breeds doing well, but also more small producers are seeing the production of heritage breeds as a way to expand their offerings to an eager consumer.

John Caveny and his wife of Caveny Farm in Monticello, Illinois, near Champaign, were among the first producers of heritage turkeys. In 2001 they raised a mere two dozen Bourbon Red turkeys and sold out immediately. Bourbon Red is their turkey of choice for its rich flavor, and they round out their bird flock with American buff geese and Rouen ducks. They have been holding at 720 birds since about 2007 because of limits in processing: in central Illinois, there are not sufficient facilities to harvest larger numbers of birds by Thanksgiving.

Caveny orders poults (as baby turkeys are called) from a hatchery at the beginning of the year. They arrive in ventilated boxes of eighty via the United States Postal Service in April. What happens next is pretty remarkable for those of us who do not know much about farm animals. It turns out that turkeys have a complex social structure, so they remain in their groups of eighty, forming a sort of clan as they peck on penned-in pasture. Some turkeys evolve into the role of guards, sticking to the perimeter of the pen and notifying the group when something is not right, and taking shifts so others can sleep. The turkey groups will not be comingled: individual turkeys have not bonded with those in other groups, so clan warfare can ensue.

"I'm no psychologist," says Caveny, "but part of raising these birds is understanding the social structure." Caveny points out that his farm experiences a low death loss and credits this in part to the understanding of turkey society and bonding behavior.

Caveny Farm's turkey pens are moved every day to provide clean grass and fresh forage. The birds get a daily feed ration free from animal protein and antibiotics, and they live like this for about seven months, compared to the twelve-week age of turkeys raised on large commercial farms. Food experts cite not only the feed but also the longer production span for the deeper, richer taste.

The comeback of heritage turkeys has not occurred in a vacuum. Slow Food, an organization that works to advance local food and small farms, is credited with saving several breeds of turkeys that are direct descendants of the country's first domesticated flocks. The heritage turkey program is part of Slow Food's Ark of Taste, named with a nod to the biblical story of Noah's Ark, where animals were saved two by two to repopulate the world. Slow Food seeks to preserve foods in danger of being lost to the influence of industrialized agriculture that favors fewer foods—ones that lend themselves to mass production but not necessarily to taste. The organizers at Slow Food initiated the heritage turkey program to help farmers find a market for these birds by connecting an eager audience with producers.

While some people want a heritage turkey purely for the flavor, others cite the environmental elements, the fact that they are contributing to biodiversity, and a closer connection to the food source, which also makes for a more interesting celebration of our nation's heritage.

The American Livestock Breeds Conservancy identifies several criteria to define a heritage turkey. First, they must be able to mate naturally. Second, they must be able to survive in nature, meaning they are able to breed in an outdoor environment and have a lifespan of about five to seven years for hens and three to five for toms, considerably longer than commercial birds. Third, they should sustain a moderate growth rate of about twenty-eight weeks, which gives the bird healthy organs and a strong skeleton. These standards are identical to the way commercial birds were raised in the first half of the twentieth century.

Getting Your Heritage Bird to the Table

With such tender, loving care and high-quality feed, these heritage turkeys do not come cheap. And that investment in your Thanksgiving table also requires a little more attention at the cooking stage.

Being free range means the turkeys develop muscle, unlike those produced in confinement facilities. And these birds have not been injected with water and oil to keep them moist, so proper cooking is key to a rich, delectable taste at dinnertime.

First, to calculate how much bird you will need, multiply the number of Thanksgiving revelers by one to one-and-a-half pounds per person. Thus, for eight people, you would likely need a turkey weighing eight to twelve pounds. If you like leftovers, order a little larger bird.

Next, get a good meat thermometer and roast at 300–325 degrees Fahrenheit until the thigh registers 180 degrees. An eight- to ten-pound bird will be ready in about two hours, but check it at an hour and 15 minutes just to be sure. Overcook these birds, and the meat will be tough and chewy—never the desired result. Be sure to let the turkey rest for about twenty minutes or so to let the juices reabsorb into the meat.

Community Supported Agriculture

Community supported agriculture—or CSA—could more accurately be called subscription farming. Members pay a fee in advance and then receive a weekly share of the harvest throughout the season. Delivery can run two ways: members can either pick up from a central location—an alderman's office, community center, or church—or they can pick up their shares at a farmers' market. The benefit to the eater is that every week they get what is freshest, and the benefit to the farmer is that they get an infusion of cash at the beginning of the season, when they need it most for seeds and supplies. Plus, they get an idea of how many families to plan for. The risk is that if bad weather ruins some crops, the harvest can lack selection and members may end up with more kale than they know what to do with.

The American CSA movement began in New England in the mid-1980s. Today, the nation's largest CSA is in the heartland. **Angelic Organics** is based in Caledonia, Illinois, about eighty miles northwest of Chicago. It has more than fourteen hundred members and drops off shares to a daunting twenty-eight sites as far west as Elgin and Geneva, and as far south as the Hyde Park neighborhood in Chicago. They have taken their mission a step further to include training for future farmers as part of Collaborative Regional Alliance for Farming Training program composed of more than twenty farms..

Angelic Organics was made famous by the 2005 Taggart Siegel film *The Real Dirt on Farmer John,* containing the memorable visual of farmer John Peterson on a tractor wearing a pink feather boa. It tells the story of how Peterson reinvented his family farm after his father died, leaving him with chief farming responsibilities when he was sixteen. Because of the upheaval of 1970s farming, he was forced to sell most of the land to pay debts; at the same time, he was disenchanted with the era's industrial approach to growing. He tells the story about attracting "hippies, radicals, and philosophers" as he transitioned his growing practices, which did not sit well with the more conservative traditionalists in his area, making him a pariah. But being shunned by the neighbors was not his only problem. While moving to organic, "we had every kind of scourge the Bible mentions," Peterson says in the film. Given the current success of his venture, it is clear his members are glad he persevered.

How to Decide If a CSA Is for You

Are you an adventurous cook? The farmer will put together a box of what's in season. If you are intrigued with trying less familiar foods, say rutabagas or celery root, membership in a CSA is your chance for a surprise every week.

Do you cook at home several days a week? Farmers have responded to the needs of smaller households by offering half shares, but some people are nevertheless frustrated with an overabundance of produce. They can be encouraged to donate their vacation shares or extra produce to underprivileged patrons.

Are you comfortable taking risks? The challenge with CSA membership is that sometimes weather conspires against the farmer, and crops fail. Most members like the idea of standing with the farmer come what may, but others are looking for peak selection, in which case the farmers' market may be their choice.

Land of Goshen Community Market

Alongside the Madison County Courthouse, the Land of Goshen Community Market gives Edwardsville residents a Saturday morning destination for food and works by artists. Start with a scone from **Queen's Cuisine**. **Backyard Beef** offers natural sausages, and **Daydream Farm**, **Sorenson Farm**, and **Looking Glass Prairie** all have free-range eggs. **Biver Farms** sells certified-organic vegetables and fruits, **Clutts Farm** sells blueberries, apples, and peaches, as well as squash, green beans, and tomatoes. **Luna Herb Company** has cherries, elderberries, grapes, wild greens, and herbs. More vendors include **Voss Pecans**, **Rensing's Pork and Beef**, **Mooney Hill Produce**, **Nuernberger's Nuts**, **SS Backwards Longhorn Meats**, and **Reinhardt's Berry Patch**. **Mills Apple Farm** serves pies and cider slush in addition to tree fruit.

Founded 1997

50+ vendors

Saturdays, May through October

St. Louis Street between Main and Second Streets, Edwardsville

Missouri is the Show Me State, and it certainly has a thing or two to show us about local food and small, diverse farms. And Missouri is no slouch when it comes to farmers' markets, either. Anchored on either end by metropolises surrounded by rich farmland, Missouri is home to distinctive, energetic individuals who are making a name for the state in local eating. A common thread among the younger set of farmers and food artisans is that they left home seeking excitement, then returned to their roots.

First, we arrive in St. Louis, with its iconic Gateway Arch designed by architect Eero Saarinen and completed in 1965, a symbol of St. Louis as the Gateway to the West. In the shadow of the arch is the Soulard Market. Its original structure was built in 1843, and the current building dates to 1929. As with many massive, permanent market buildings, its storied past ebbs and flows with the evolution of American cities. It was closed in the 1940s, as were many markets, but reopened in the 1970s, and today it is predominantly a brokers' market, with bananas and pine-apples side by side with regional foods.

Tower Grove Farmers' Market

40 vendors

Saturdays, May through November

Northwest Drive and Central Cross Drive, Tower Grove Park, St. Louis

Visit Tower Grove Park on a Saturday morning, and you can come away perfectly balanced by filling your canvas bag with delicious food and practicing yoga with like-minded shoppers. Every Saturday, weather permitting, you will see several dozen yoga mats—as many as one hundred—arranged in a circle on the grass, the yogis going through sun salutations, an ancient series of poses that greet the morning and leave practitioners set for the day. "Buying food at the farmers market is a holistic way to buy food, and yoga is a holistic way to take care of your body," says Keith Mitchell, who instructs the free sessions on Saturday mornings.

Tower Grove Park itself is an inspiring site. The out-buildings capture a distinct sense of time and place, and I thought that if I squinted I could almost see a scene from the end of "Meet Me In St. Louis," the 1944 musical where Judy Garland and Margaret O'Brien strolled the 1904 world's fair in oversized white hats and fluffy white Edwardian dresses. The park predates the fair—it was established in 1868, a gift from Henry Shaw, a philanthropist who also founded the Missouri Botanic Garden. Shaw had come to St. Louis in 1819 as a teenager and became a successful businessman selling hardware, tools, and cutlery to farmers and immigrant settlers. After a twenty-year career, he retired at age forty and pursued his interest in botany.

The farmers' market is housed on a patio near the 1914 pool pavilion resembling a Greek temple. Vendors are lined up in aisles, with more along the path to the meandering road that goes through the park. The pavilion presides over a wading pool, great for kids and for cooling off on a steamy day.

Farmers at Tower Grove

» Back in 1821, when James Monroe was president, Leonard Harold established **Centennial Farms** and also founded the town of Augusta on his own property. A few decades later he sold acreage to Christian Knoernschild. Centennial Farms remains in the Knoernschild family today, where six generations later, the family grandsons live on the farm. Current owners Bob and Ellen Knoernschild planted orchards and vines in the 1960s and now have more than 1,400 fruit trees in addition to the berry and vegetable plantings on their farm. The Knoernschilds sell at the market and also have their own farm market from July through November, when visitors can tour the farm and buy fresh food as well as honey, four kinds of apple butter, and more than a dozen varieties of preserves. The original log cabin is restored, and the farmstead is listed on the National Register of Historic Places. When high summer comes, Ellen Knoernschild recommends pureeing their peaches and mixing with vanilla ice cream.

» Aaron and Agi Groff of **4 Seasons Baked Goods** were both classically trained at the Culinary Institute of America. They sell an array of delectables (even dog treats) at Tower Grove as well as two other markets.

Aaron Groff of 4 Seasons Baked Goods

» Food artisan and St. Louis native son Mark Sanfilippo of **Salume Beddu** fell in love with Italian-style cured meats as a student in Germany. "I spent a year in Germany, and the school housed international students by nationality," he says. "My last name is Italian, so I was mixed in with the Italian students."

Those Italian students would return from weekends home with salami and prosciutto made in their parents' basements, and Sanfilippo was smitten. Years later, as an aspiring screenwriter, Sanfilippo worked with Mario

Batali, the redheaded, ponytailed TV chef most recognized for wearing shorts and orange Crocs in all weather. Batali has had programs on the Food Network and Public Television and comes by his love of cured meats honestly because his father, Armandino Batali, is a nationally recognized salume artisan based in Seattle. Sanfilippo answered a classified ad for staff at Pizzeria Mozza, Batali's restaurant with co-owner and artisan baker Nancy Silverton.

Marco Sanfillipo of Salume Beddu

"I think I got the job because I asked a lot of questions and was excited about the idea of curing meats," said Sanfilippo. With his vision focused, he knew he needed to get back to the Midwest. "I realized that the meat we were working with came from Missouri and Iowa, and I decided St. Louis would be a good place for a business."

Sanfilippo and his wife, another St. Louis native, made the move back home, and Sanfilippo began creating his own brand of cured meats. The name of his business translates from Italian to "beautiful cured meats." And beautiful they are. Business partner Ben Poremba joined the team in 2008.

Sanfilippo's business is another example of using farmers' markets as an incubator, to create and sell products and develop a clientele before opening a brick-and-mortar shop. Salume Beddu opened in mid-2010.

» Next door to Salume Beddu is third-generation producer Dave Hillebrand of **Prairie Grass Farm**, which produces about seven hundred lambs and six hundred chickens a year, all free range. His farm in New Florence, about halfway in between St. Louis and Columbia, has been the site of the annual Lambstravaganza, where seven chefs and several hundred guests descend on the farm to enjoy good food and raise money for Slow Food's micro-grant program. Billed as "a feast in the field," the event gathers diners at one long table; the proceeds go to farmers who produce heirloom and heritage foods, helping them purchase seeds, equipment, and livestock.

» When joining the long line at **Ivan's Fig Farm**, it is important to understand one thing. Figs do not grow in the Midwest: our icy winters kill the trees. Only a few years ago, local Missouri figs would have indicated an agriculture miracle. But Ivan Stoilov missed the fruit of his native Bulgaria and found a way to grow his favorite by installing enormous greenhouses to create what's essentially an indoor orchard, a totally self-sustaining operation heated by solar and geothermal power. Stoilov studied at Stanford University in California and came to his ten acres in Missouri in 1995.

Dave Hillebrand of Prairie Grass Farm

» **Ringhausen Orchards** is heading toward its sixth generation. When I met Joe Ringhausen, who represents the fourth generation, and his wife Sina, they were selling with their grandson Alex, who may become the sixth generation of fruit growers in Fielden and Jerseyville. Ringhausen grows eight to ten varieties each of apples and peaches, selecting early-, mid-, and late-season varieties in order to have fruit that ripens all season long.

» At Tower Grove you will also find **City Seeds Urban Farm**, which teaches job skills to people who perhaps have not seen many fresh vegetables prior to joining the program, as well as **Greenwood Farms**, a pasture-raised meat and poultry farm that bills itself "the solution to the omnivore's dilemma," referring to the landmark book by Michael Pollan that explores how food is raised today. The **Kuva Coffee Company** has direct relationships with its bean growers. **Biver Farms** and **Double Star Farms** are only two of the go-to stands for vegetables.

Ferguson Farmers' Market

Founded 2002

40+ vendors

Saturdays, April through October

20 South Florissant Road, Ferguson

Located in the heart of the Ferguson Citywalk district, a vibrant community filled with historic buildings, the farmers' market is a highlight of Saturday mornings for Ferguson residents. Visit **Siebert Farms** for organic meats and double-yolk eggs, **Kamp's Orchard** for peaches, **R. W. Martin Farms** for a luscious array of melons, **Seventh Generation Farm** for greens and other vegetables, **Thies Farm** for strawberries, red all the way through. Try local pasta at **Papardelle's**, and choose from tomato cracked pepper papardelle, basil garlic fettuccine, or spinach angel hair. For a snack while you shop, stop by the omelet stand, or try a grilled pizza from **"R" Pizza Farm**.

Ferguson vendor John Wilkerson is a new farmer, despite gray hair and a face that radiates wisdom. He took up his new profession after a career in computers; he leases land from the Mueller Farm, which has been in cultivation since 1883.

Like so many growers, Molly Rockamann came to farming via a circuitous route. Eager to branch out from her St. Louis suburban roots, she studied organic growing at University of California at Santa Cruz, then did research on Fiji, where she helped a grower of sugar cane, one of the most chemically intensive crops, transition to organic.

Eventually, however, home called, and Rockamann found herself back in St. Louis with the family business, living at home and socking away her salary with plans to start EarthDance, a vision that goes deeper than farming, exploring the connection to our world that encompasses culture and art in addition to beans and tomatoes. Even the name of her operation, **EarthDance FARMS**, stands for Food, Arts, Relationships, Music—Sustainability! with an exclamation point for emphasis. In addition to their presence at the market, EarthDance sells to restaurants, including FarmHaus, Sellina Pasta Café, and Acero.

John Wilkerson is a second-career farmer at Mueller Farm

Maplewood Farmers' Market, Schlafly Bottleworks

The Maplewood Market at the go-to local brewery in St. Louis offers a midweek treat for local food fans. Vendors include **4 Seasons Baked Goods**, **Baetje Farms**, **Black Bear Bakery**, **Blue Heron Orchard**, **Centennial Farms**, **El Chico Bakery**, **Esther's Honey**, **Farrar Out Farm**, **Grandma's Nuts**, **Ivan's Fig Farm**, **Kakao Chocolates**, **Missouri Grass Fed Beef**, **Murray's Orchard**, **Ozark Forest Mushroom**, **Salume Beddu**, **Silent Oaks Farm**, and **Sunflower Savannah**. The **Marcoot Jersey Creamery** is a seventh-generation family farm, milking sixty cows in Greenville, Illinois.

Brian DeSmet was bitten by the food bug when he returned to St. Louis after a few years of living in New York. He is one of those multitasking individuals with three jobs making the world safe for sustainable agriculture. Not only does he manage the Maplewood Market every Wednesday at the Schlafly Bottleworks, he is also the newest manager of Tower Grove Farmers' Market, assisting market director Patrick Horine. In addition, DeSmet works with the St. Louis Farmers' Market Association, a relatively new organization supported by the Missouri Department of Agriculture. His mission there is to help streamline processes, like permitting, to help farmers' markets thrive without putting a burden on farmers who drive in to sell.

The good folks at Schlafly beer, the local brewery of St. Louis, put their money where their mouths are when it comes to supporting the local food in the region. They host the Maplewood Market in their parking lot, and they donate to Slow Food St. Louis events, like Lambstravaganza.

25+ vendors

Wednesdays, April through October

7260 Southwest Avenue, Maplewood

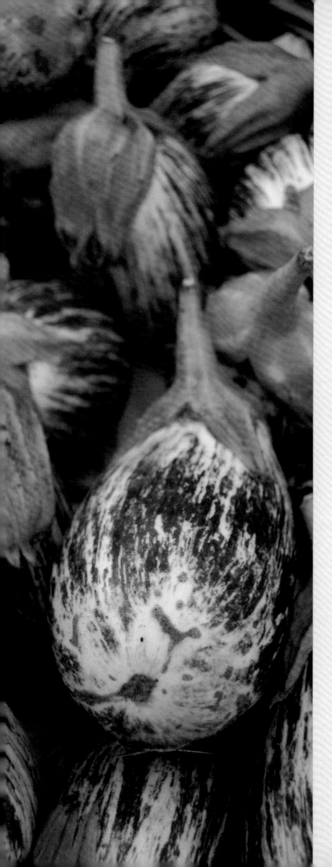

Caterer Julie Ridlon realized the St. Louis area was losing farms at an alarming rate. She decided an upscale farmers' market was the means to generate enough volume purchases to make it worth it for the farmers to make the trek into the city.

"Too many farms were folding," she said, and goes on to describe that she wanted to create a market where people could buy all their produce for the week. In 1999 she founded the Clayton Farmers' Market with a volunteer committee. The market now is run by a grocery store, but Ridlon still serves as a tireless advocate for local food. She is outspoken about restaurants jumping on the farmers' market bandwagon without the chops to back it up. "We find chefs who are tempted to buy the bulk of their ingredients from wholesalers and buy the garnish at the farmers' market just so they can say they shop local," said Ridlon. She says restaurant patrons can play a role by asking about where the ingredients come from.

Ridlon says what is great about her caponata is that it can be almost any amount of eggplant, squash, and peppers to suit your personal taste and will last in the fridge for a couple of weeks. Serve it as a salad, sandwich filling, or dip with pita chips. Ridlon likes it served with chèvre on toasted baguette.

Caponata: Italian Eggplant Salad

Julie Ridlon, Chanterelle Catering

2 tablespoons olive oil

3 medium onions, peeled and chopped (red or yellow)

3 cloves garlic, peeled and minced

1 large eggplant or 4 smaller eggplants (peel half the skin with a potato peeler and leave the rest for texture), cut into ½-inch cubes

3–4 summer squash cut into ½-inch cubes (try any combination of zucchini, zephyr, or crookneck)

1–2 red, yellow, or orange peppers, seeded and cut into cubes

2 stalks of celery, cut into ½-inch pieces

Salt and pepper to taste

¼ cup apple cider vinegar

1–2 tablespoons brown sugar

1 teaspoon fresh thyme

1 teaspoon chili flakes (optional)

3 large tomatoes, peeled and diced

½ cup raisins (use golden or dark raisins, or currants)

¼ cup capers drained, or ⅓ cup pitted calamata olives

8 large basil leaves, thinly sliced

Sauté the onion, garlic, eggplant, squash, peppers, and celery for eight to ten minutes, stirring occasionally, until fork tender. Depending on the ripeness of the vegetables, it may take an additional five to ten minutes. Season with salt and pepper.

As the vegetables cook, whisk together the cider vinegar, brown sugar, thyme, and chili flakes (if using) in a small bowl. Toss together in a large bowl the tomatoes, raisins, capers (or olives), and basil. Stir in cooked eggplant mixture, and taste for balance, adding additional vinegar, salt, or sugar. Store tightly covered in the refrigerator.

Slow Food: Founded on the Philosophy of "Enough Already"

We have talked about a few Slow Food initiatives, like saving heritage poultry with the American Livestock Breeds Conservancy in Ohio and heritage turkeys in the Illinois chapter. Missouri seems a great place to go more in depth because the St. Louis convivium, as each local chapter is called, has made a grand gesture in support of local food by creating a micro-grant program for local growers, which can help farmers move forward to add heritage animal breeds and heirloom plant varieties to their offerings at a time when a financial risk can be daunting.

Slow Food was founded in 1986 in Italy when a McDonald's opened at the foot of the Spanish Steps in Rome. Journalist Carlo Petrini essentially stood up, shook his fist, and declared "basta." Enough. He said, "We don't want fast food, we want slow food." Protesters organized demonstrations where Italian celebrities like Sophia Loren served heaping bowls of pasta to showcase traditional foods. A quarter century later Slow Food has become a worldwide movement devoted to small farms, local food, and preserving food culture in the face of the globalization of our food systems.

One of Slow Food's key initiatives is Terra Madre, a bi-annual gathering of farmers and chefs in Turin, Italy. The first Terra Madre was held in 2004 and was deemed an eye opener for farmers who heard fellow delegates say, "We don't feel alone anymore." Delegates stay as guests of the host country and are often entertained to multicourse meals, complete with local wine, after a day's sessions held in a facility originally built for the winter Olympics in 2006.

Upon returning, delegates report a lot of learning and tasting, but they seem most proud of the recognition. From here forward, these growers are referred to as Terra Madre delegates. It is a badge of honor that puts them at the top of their game.

Another Slow Food program is the Ark of Taste. In keeping with the biblical story where Noah saved species from an epic flood, the Ark of Taste strives to catalog foods at risk and create a plan to save them. The most successful of these is the heritage turkey program in tandem with the American Livestock Breeds Conservancy. But there is also a movement afoot to save the paw paw, the luscious fruit that fell out of favor, which was discussed on page 28.

Pony Express Farmers' Market

In 1860, the first pony express rider left St. Joseph to deliver mail to the West. The service lasted only nineteen months, but St. Joseph residents embrace their heritage. Enjoy some great vegetables from **River Bluff Produce**, **Mackey Farms**, **L & R Farms**, **Hill Farms Produce**, and **Old Ott Farms**, which grows organically. Stop by **Jirak Family Produce** for sweet corn. Get artisan cheese from **Nannie Cheese**. **Blazerfarmz** sell products made with aroniaberry, said to have good antioxidant properties. Grab a snack from **The Enchilada Lady**.

20 vendors

Wednesdays and Saturdays, April through October

East Ridge Village, Frederick Avenue and Village Drive, St. Joseph

Jackson Farmers' Market

Get vegetables from **Sunset Ridge Farms**, **Brumleve Farm**, **Mike Onderdonk**, **Clay Birk**, and **Bob Ulrich**, and eggs and meat from **Janzow Farms**. **Gihring Family Farm** sells maple syrup, goat milk, naturally grown produce and whole wheat baked goods. Buy berries from **Bryan's Berry Patch**. **Show Me Fresh Farm** features herbs and preserves in addition to produce. **Cindy Ingram**, **Chesser Family Farm**, and **Mary Bowers** bring the baked goods.

20+ vendors

Tuesdays and Saturdays, May through October

Jackson City Park, Route D, Jackson

USDA's Farmers' Market Promotion Program, and How to Grow Your Farm

As farmers' markets are exploding, even the United States Department of Agriculture is getting into the act. Once known only for doling out large subsidies to commodity crop producers, the USDA has expanded the Farmers' Market Promotion Program.

In 2002, the USDA dedicated funds to promote farmers' markets and began a grant program. In 2010, when I was a reviewer, USDA distributed $5 million in grants. By 2011, the figure rose to $10 million. Granted, it does not come anywhere near the billions in crop subsidies and food assistance the USDA provides, but it is a start, and it demonstrates that the government is looking at many ways to help people eat healthier.

Debi Kelly, an extension agent with the University of Missouri, told me about the university's fantastic **Grow Your Farm** program, made possible in part by a substantial grant from the USDA. Students in the program learn to walk their property to assess their needs and resources and then draw a farmstead map, which considers the watershed and topography. "We look at everything," she says. "For example, what is the slope on your property? If you want to farm organically and your neighbor farm uses chemicals, how will you prevent chemicals from running onto your soil? And if you want a U-pick operation, will your customers be able to find you five miles down a gravel road?"

One of the things Kelly believes sets Grow Your Farm apart from other farm training programs is that novice growers get a mentor, an established farmer who helps them through the process. "The biggest take-away is relationships," says Kelly. "People who go through the program have found people they can count on for years to come."

Grow Your Farm also puts farmers through their paces by requiring them to create business plans for their farms. "Farming is a business. The farmers who know that they have clients, that they need a marketing plan, that they need to utilize their resources effectively are the ones who are going to be more successful," says Kelly's colleague Shelley Bush Rowe, a community development specialist with the University of Missouri Extension. Over the past four to five years, Grow Your Farm has trained about eighty farmers. Debi Kelly's favorite market is in her hometown of Columbia.

Greater Springfield Farmers' Market

Springfield hosts the largest producer market in Missouri and limits vendors to a seventy-mile radius. Start with a little caffeine from **Copper Canyon Coffee Roasters**. Get grapes at **Dove Mountain Organic Vineyard**, edamame and Asian vegetables from **Echigo Farm**, berries, melons and vegetables from **Jensen Gardens**, and just about everything from **Millsap Farms** and **Morning Glory Farm**. Find meat at **Middleton's All Natural Meats**, **Ozarks Natural Foods**, **Flintrock Bison Ranch**, and **Burton's Farm**. For baked goods get authentic French macaroons from **Farm Girl Bakery**, granola from **Granolove**, pie from **Sunshine Valley Farm**, and artisan breads from **Deeper Roots Farm** and **Black Owl Bread Company**. The four-leggers can fetch a treat from **All God's Creatures Dog Bakery**.

Founded 1978

100 vendors

Tuesdays, Thursdays, and Saturdays, May through October

Battlefield Mall parking lot, Battlefield Road and Glenstone Avenue, Springfield

Columbia Farmers' Market

Travel west of St. Louis about 125 miles and you arrive at Columbia, home to the University of Missouri and a farmers' market located outside the posh Activity and Recreation Center, known as ARC. Producers at this market travel from a mere fifty-four-mile radius, a near distance difficult in large cities like Chicago, where suburbs and small towns can stretch the urban rim almost that far. Plans are in the works for a farmers' market pavilion, but in the meantime shoppers can stroll a line of tents with vendors selling every possible food.

More than one person told me that "Columbia has the best market in Missouri"—bold words for a state

Founded 1980

90 vendors

Mondays, Wednesdays, and Saturdays, May through October

Activity and Recreation Center (ARC) parking lot, 1701 Ash Street, Columbia that seems to have preserved a great deal of small, diversified farms. Here, at least eight vendors have eggs, and six carry meat. **Sandy Creek Farm** sells pecans and twenty-three varieties of peaches. You can score spring-raised rainbow trout from **Troutdale Farm** and take home honey ice cream from **Walk-About Acres**. The lone cheese vendor is **Goatsbeard Farm**, where Ken and Jenn Munro make an array of farmstead cheeses.

One diversified farm that sells at Columbia is **Chert Hollow Farm**. Owner Eric Reuter comes to the market with berries, mushrooms, and a wide variety of vegetables and herbs. Even the farm's name is steeped in a sense of place. "Chert is a geologic term for the rock known as flint, and hollow is the Ozark term for valley," explains Reuter, who waxes poetic about a life lived outdoors. Both he and his wife, Joanna, are serious cooks and strive to "leave the land better than we found it," he says.

The Reuters keep dairy goats for their own use, as well as geese and a pig, although they do not sell meat, poultry, or dairy products at the market. To sell goat cheese at the farmers' market, they would need a licensed dairy facility, which would set them back about $50,000. But they embrace the symbiotic process of having animals on the farm. The animals graze on land not suitable for vegetable production and in turn help fertilize with their waste.

Chert Hollow is certified organic by MOSA, the Midwest Organic Services Association, a nonprofit organization based in Viroqua, Wisconsin, not far from LaFarge, the home of the Organic Valley family of farms, and has been called a model organic farm for the area. High praise indeed for Chert Hollow, a farm that began in 2006.

Janine's Rosemary Sea Salt Shortbread

Cooking with herbs is an integral way to accentuate flavor. At the Columbia market, you can buy herbs at **Harvester**, **Donllinger Farm**, **God's Green Earth**, *and* **Kea International Market**, *which specializes in Korean and Vietnamese vegetables.*

I find that one of the best ways to showcase fresh herbs is to serve them up in surprising ways. Rosemary shortbread has become my signature holiday cookie.

MAKES 16 TRIANGLES

8 tablespoons (1 stick) unsalted butter, room temperature

¼ cup sugar

1 teaspoon coarse sea salt, plus extra for sprinkling

2 tablespoons minced fresh rosemary, plus extra for sprinkling

1 cup all-purpose flour

Preheat oven to 325 degrees. Stir together the butter, sugar, and salt, then stir in the rosemary. Mix in half the flour, then add remaining flour and combine. The dough may become stiff, so be patient. Press into an eight-inch square pan and sprinkle with a little extra rosemary and salt for a pretty finish. Use a fork to pierce dough at one-inch intervals. Bake until lightly golden around the edges, about thirty minutes. Remove from oven and immediately cut into triangles. Cool for about five minutes, then promptly remove shortbread from pan using offset spatula or fork.

City Market, Kansas City

Founded 1857; current farmers' market since 1970s

140 vendors

Saturdays and Sundays all year; first Wednesdays, May through October

Fifth and Walnut Streets, Kansas City, Missouri

Missouri's western metropolis, Kansas City, is where you will find an enthusiastic chef who gave up surfing in Hawaii to put a stake in the ground for farm-to-table eating in the Midwest. Chef/owner Michael Foust of The Farmhouse serves up local fare from a half dozen local farms, including **Goode Acres**, which sells at the City Market in downtown Kansas City. "I thought I'd be competing with every restaurant in town for food from area growers," Foust says. Not so. Even though he is a relative newcomer to the Kansas City restaurant scene, he is at the forefront of the farm-to-table philosophy in the city where he has built relationships with a number of producers, going so far as to buy a pig whose genetics he appreciates and then transfer the piglet, in a cat carrier, to a farm whose no-grain feeding philosophy matches his own. He has even broken the never-name-your-dinner policy (serious meat producers never name animals). When I asked what he named the piglet, Foust said, "Dinner." I could not help but think of a friend who named her backyard chickens Pot Pie and Kung Pao.

Foust is a fixture at the City Market, which has a long, storied history, dating back to the 1850s. The area boomed during the railroad era, then later deteriorated, and then boomed again in the 1930s and 1940s. In 1941 the Kansas City Star reported that the market was responsible for one thousand jobs. Then decline hit again, as with most urban neighborhoods. But in recent decades people have gravitated toward cities, and the City Market has enjoyed the boon of people moving into condos and lofts near downtown, ethnic populations who grew up with open-air markets as their source for food and people who just enjoy fresh food. Because City Market draws so many ethnic groups, vendor **Barbara Flores** does a thriving business in live chickens, the only live animal vendor

Chef/owner Michael Foust of The Farmhouse

Pulled Pork Sliders with Apple and Smoked Pepper Salad

Michael Foust, The Farmhouse

MAKES 12 SLIDERS

2½ pounds pork butt

1- 2 tablespoons apple cider vinegar

¼ teaspoon salt, or to taste

¼ teaspoon freshly ground black pepper, or to taste

Apple and smoked pepper salad (recipe follows)

12 small dinner rolls (about three inches wide)

Wrap pork twice in heavy-duty aluminum foil and place in baking dish. Cook at 300 degrees until very tender, up to six hours, but start checking at three hours because timing can vary dramatically. You know the meat is ready when it pulls apart easily with your fingers. Remove from oven, cool for a few minutes, then shred by hand. You will have about four cups of pulled pork. Drizzle with vinegar and sprinkle with salt and pepper.

The companion flavors of apples and pork shine here in tiny sandwiches from Chef Michael Foust. Use whatever apple is fresh off the tree: both tart and sweet varieties go well in this dish. It is best to make the pork the day before to ensure tenderness: shred it before you assemble the sandwiches.

Apple and Smoked Pepper Salad

2 tablespoons sherry vinegar

½ teaspoon honey

1 smoked red chili, minced

½ teaspoon finely chopped fresh sage

Salt and pepper to taste

3 apples

¼ cup black walnut pieces, toasted

Whisk together the vinegar and honey in a large mixing bowl, then toss in the chili and sage. Season with salt and pepper. Cut the apple away from the core, then slice julienne style, leaving the skin on. Add the apples and walnuts to the salad dressing and toss to coat. Let marinate for about thirty minutes before assembling the sliders.

To assemble, split the rolls horizontally and place the bottoms on a tray. Scoop about ⅓ cup of the pulled pork onto each bottom half, then divide the apple salad among the sandwiches. Top off with the rest of the bun halves and serve immediately.

Deb Connors is market manager at the City Market in Kansas City

I discovered on my trip. "Some people like their chickens really fresh," said market manager Deb Connors. I find myself wondering if we will return to a time when people process their own chickens, including the arduous process of plucking.

At City Market, visit **Fahrmeier Farm** for pumpkins, cantaloupe, and watermelon; **Lost Creek Farm** for chickens, potatoes, and cabbage; and **Bryson's Farm Fresh Produce** for berries and tomatoes. Other vendors include **KC Buffalo**, **Windy Ridge Greenhouse & Produce**, **Bad Seed Farm**, **Strawberry Lane Farm**, and **Peacock Farm**.

The City Market started electronic benefits transfer in 2009, and organizers are encouraged at the enthusiastic response. In the first year, the market had $8,000 in redemptions, compared to a total of about $12,000 for the entire state of Missouri, said Connors. Next up: a mobile market, essentially a van outfitted to sell meat, eggs, and produce to five or six neighborhoods that may have residents who cannot make it to the market. The market also received a USDA Farmers' Market Promotion Program grant to install a commercial kitchen. The grant (more than $67,000) is being matched by the city—a hefty budget in terms of a kitchen remodel, but the commercial kitchen can be used by entrepreneurs starting food companies to experiment with product development, by farmers who want to preserve their harvest by making sauces, and also for cooking demonstrations at the market. In the works: property manager Deb Churchill is getting bids for exhaust systems and three-compartment sinks required for a commercial facility, as well as all the other elements of a professional kitchen.

Independence Farmers' Market

Independence, Missouri, home of Harry Truman and the seat of Jackson County, wins the prize for the earliest market open. By 5:00 A.M. growers are positioned in a parking lot within walking distance from the Jackson County Courthouse, marked by a statue of President Truman himself stepping out on one of his walks. Vendors range from Ralph and John Payne, a father-and-son team from **Payne Farm** with a wide-ranging display of every imaginable vegetable; to Louis Perez of **Perez Peppers**, brother- and son-in-law to the Paynes, with a large selection of peppers and other Hispanic vegetables; to Peggy Waring, who sells fruit from her twelve-tree

Founded circa 1971

40 vendors

Wednesdays, June through October; Saturdays, May through October

Independence Square, between Truman Road and Main Street, Independence

Peggy Waring sells fruit from her twelve-tree orchard

John and Ralph Payne sell at the Independence Market

orchard and declines to call herself a "real" farmer because of the intimate nature of her operation. But the Black Arkansas apples, tart and extra-firm, make a mighty nice pie. **Graybill's Produce** has a wide variety of squashes. Other vendors include **Adams Produce**, **Brad Hall Farm**, **Jenkins Produce**, **Happy Rooster Farm**, **Berry Nut Jams**, **Beckner Orchard** and **Thomas Farms**. Market manager is the affable Joe Antoine, owner of **Antoine Seed**, a company that sells seed to both farmers and home gardeners.

How to Have a Rocking Farmers' Market

Farmers' markets have become so popular that some hopefuls think of them as the key to a bustling town center. Although a vibrant farmers' market can add cachet and foot traffic, a new market is almost never an instant success. Some of the more successful markets struggled for several seasons. If you have aspirations to start a farmers' market, keep these factors in mind:

Location, location, location. Leafy parks and courthouse squares make for the most desirable settings, but a central location with easy access and free parking trumps everything. I found people who would drive five miles out of their way because a another nearby market only had paid parking.

The glitter of celebrity. Whether your local celebs are chefs, politicians, or business leaders, you need people to lend their endorsement. Cooking demonstrations by chefs and cooking school instructors can help drive traffic and awareness.

A committee that delivers. Some markets foundered when all the organizers were food people who came to the venture with passion but a narrow skill set. A strong market needs financial management, an organized volunteer program, and someone astute at navigating city ordinances. Educational programming and entertainment are a big plus, but fundraising is by far the biggest contributor to success.

Energetic volunteers. A number of markets were all volunteer, with no operating budget aside from in-kind contributions. But even if yours gets support from a municipality or other organization, you will need volunteers to staff an information table, help with marketing initiatives, write grant proposals, and organize fundraisers and other events.

Civic engagement. Your municipality can help you navigate permits and come to your ribbon cutting.

Herbert Hoover's birthplace, West Branch, Iowa

Iowa

I enter Iowa on a drenched day by crossing the mighty Mississippi River. Driving east on I-80, which bisects the state, I find farmers' markets, big and small, that tell the story of this place. Even in the blustery drear, I am struck by the vibrant russet colors of the Iowa autumn.

As I make my way across the wide state, thinking about how our country feeds itself, I came across a little-remembered story on my visit to West Branch, the birthplace of Herbert Hoover and site of his presidential library. It turns out that before he was president, he had a successful international engineering career with a mining company. He found himself in London in 1914 when World War I broke out. Having established for himself a reputation for logistics, and at the request of the U.S. ambassador to Great Britain, Hoover deployed five hundred volunteers to coordinate food and travel for more than 120,000 Americans stranded in Europe. He later orchestrated a relief effort for Belgium, whose citizens were trapped in fighting between England and Germany. The museum is filled with flour sacks that Belgians embroidered with messages of thanks to Mr. Hoover.

After my flag-waving respite I hopped back in the car, only to be detoured again in Grinnell, home to a great college and one of the few remaining banks designed by famed architect Louis Sullivan. Some of the students shopping at the farmers' market told me how they plan an all-local Thanksgiving with heritage turkeys raised by a music instructor.

Next I circled around Des Moines to check out Winterset, which has a market on the square. Movie buffs will remember it as the setting for the film *The Bridges of Madison County*, starring Meryl Streep and Clint Eastwood.

The wow-factor market is in Des Moines, the state capitol and the site of what may be one of the largest farmers' markets in the country. It is one of those markets with so many vendors that it is easy to feel overwhelmed, yet even the near-freezing temperature did nothing to dampen the enthusiasm of shoppers.

Downtown Des Moines Farmers' Market

Founded 1976

200 vendors

Saturdays, May through October, Court Avenue between Fifth Avenue and First Street

Wednesdays, late August through early October, Thirteenth Street between Grand Avenue and Locust Street

Third weekends (Fridays and Saturdays) in November and December, 400 Locust Street (Capitol Square/Nollen Plaza), Des Moines

The Downtown Des Moines Farmers' Market dates to 1976, when it had fewer than a dozen vendors and maybe two hundred shoppers. Today it runs nine city blocks down Court Avenue under the watch of the Polk County Courthouse, with hundreds of vendors on either side of the wide street and branching off onto side streets like legs on a millipede. More than eighteen thousand shoppers show up on warm Saturdays; attendance ballooned to thirty thousand on opening day in 2009. The market is operated by the Downtown Community Alliance, a nonprofit organization designed to promote a vibrant downtown. Even on a chilly day, you can see that the effort is clearly working.

In a state known for its focus on corn and hogs, the market here is remarkable in its diversity: berries, cheese from goats and cows, cultivated mushrooms, honey, even rye whiskey barbecue sauce. And the Des Moines Market has what few others have: a parking ramp. In an era where car is king, easy parking makes a difference in the success of a market.

The market also has two other essential ingredients for success: pastries and locally roasted coffee. I arrive at dawn, desperate for fuel. At the top of the market, near the courthouse, I meet Austrian immigrant Mike Leo, a baker doing a brisk business selling cookies. If the line is any indication, his **Strudl Haus Bakery** is the way he is living the American dream of coming to a new country and starting a business. Close by is **Iowa Coffee Company**, where Tom Sibbernsen sells hot coffee and is particularly popular on chilly days.

I meet up with market director Kelly Foss, who is clearly a market booster, sprinkling in news and data while introducing me to vendors by name. She gives me a guided tour and chats about the broad range of vendors, about programs to help farmers, and about organizations that help feed the needy, like the popular **Meals from the Market**,

Kelly Foss is market manager at the Des Moines Market

The Des Moines Market stretches five blocks from the courthouse

which launched in 2008. The program solicits food donations at the market, an ideal outlet for farmers who have not sold all their food, and shoppers are invited to donate food or cash as well. Foss is not the only booster. At the **Buy Fresh, Buy Local** booth, Drake University students invite people to pledge to increase their purchases of local food to 5 percent.

Farther down Court Avenue is Matt Russell of **Coyote Run Farm**, who says he did not set out to be a farmer, although you certainly cannot tell by the array of meat, eggs, and vegetables for sale at his table. And if you are in the market for a donkey, Russell is your man, along with his partner in farming and life, Patrick Standley.

Matt Russell of Coyote Run Farm

The challenge facing Matt Russell on this weekend is that he does not have enough eggs to sell. Iowans love the eggs at Coyote Run, and they may never have enough. "We brought sixty dozen to market, and we were sold out by nine o'clock," said he says. "Then we brought 120 dozen eggs, and we still sold out." Their goal is to have three hundred laying hens, a mix of the Gold Star and Red Star breeds.

They have approached farming the old-fashioned way, improving it bit by bit rather than getting a big loan and making improvements all at once. "If we'd done everything at once, we would have wasted a lot of money," says Russell. He is proud of what Iowa has accomplished in the realm of local food systems. "We have a deep and talented staff working with rural development organizations," he says, pointing to Practical Farmers of Iowa, the Leopold Center for Sustainable Agriculture, and the Drake Forum as being among the groups making a difference for small farmers today.

A few booths down from Coyote Run is **Blue Gate Farm**, which might be one of the quickest agriculture start-ups in the history of the market. Sean Skeehan and his wife, Jill Beebout, moved to their forty acres in April 2005 and were at the Downtown Des Moines Market four weeks later.

Industrial Eggs: A Cautionary Tale

Farm eggs are a great illustration of why small-scale farming has won the hearts of consumers. To understand why farm eggs are worth the money requires an understanding of why conventional eggs are so cheap, and the chilling repercussions of a food system focused solely on price. Although Iowa has many diversified farms, it is also home to some of the egg industry's largest confinement facilities.

In 2010 more than 550 *million* eggs were recalled after testing positive for *salmonella enteritidis*. The contaminated eggs caused more than sixteen hundred reported illnesses, the largest since the Centers for Disease Control began tracking salmonella in the 1970s. The eggs came from two facilities in Iowa—Wright County Farms and Hillandale Farms. These facilities—I hesitate to call them farms—are massive. About 7.7 million hens are stacked in cages that damage their feet, but the open grates make the droppings easier to sweep up (although pity the poor hen at the bottom of the stack). The hens are closely contained in battery cages, where they cannot spread their wings or move around. At a hearing called by the U.S. House of Representatives, representatives from the FDA showed photos of piles of decomposing chickens and manure so high the door of the barn could not be closed. The list of violations goes on, and one of the perpetrators had already paid millions of dollars in fines for mistreatment of workers and hiring undocumented workers.

The grim reality of industrial food production points to a widening gap where consumers concerned with stewardship of animals, earth, and people believe they have fewer choices at the supermarket.

What was on their market table? "Mostly food we begged and borrowed from our relatives," said Skeehan, noting that it is all in keeping with market guidelines because the relatives farm adjacent property. Now Skeehan and Beebout have a thirty-six-member CSA and a market table groaning under the weight of vegetables, honey, and jam, all from the family acreage.

Judy Henry of Berry Patch Farm

Their beginnings were not as miraculous as the timing might suggest, though. Their land is leased from Beebout's family, and they had done considerable planning. Skeehan describes their Certified Naturally Grown practices as going beyond organic. No chemicals are used at Blue Gate, not even organic fertilizers, and pest control mechanisms are approved by the USDA organic program. A while back Blue Gate had a situation that illustrates the tenuous relationship between organic and chemical farms. A neighbor farmer was away and hired someone to spray for him who was not aware that a chemical-free farm was next door. With winds too high to safely spray, the man sprayed anyway. When Skeehan tells the story, his voice remains even, without the raised voice or indignant manner one would expect. After all, farmers work very hard to establish reputations and credibility.

Almost next to Blue Gate we meet Judy Henry of **Berry Patch Farm**. She has been selling at this market for more than thirty-five years. She grows berries with her husband and son in Nevada, about twenty-five miles northeast of Des Moines.

Scott Bush of Templeton Rye

Scott Bush of **Templeton Rye** sells barbecue sauce made from his signature distilled beverage, once reputed to be a favorite of infamous bootlegging gangster Al Capone. "Before we realized we couldn't serve alcohol here, we gave out whiskey samples," he says. "I was surprised about all the little white-haired ladies lining up for a tipple on Saturday morning."

The prized Templeton Rye small batch is distilled right in Templeton, about eighty miles northwest of Des Moines. A larger facility in Indiana distills larger batches. Still, it is not that easy to come by. And it is a great success story of five guys coming together to relaunch a venerated beverage. Bush's partner, Michael Killmer, claims the barbecue sauce recipe as his own.

Midwest Manhattan

Templeton Rye is the perfect golden whiskey straight up or, in this classic cocktail, set off by cherries from my home state of Michigan, steeped in a boozy concoction created by Daniel Sviland, mixologist for Prairie Fire in Chicago. The cherries are best steeped in the fridge for about six weeks, but even a few days will give them a nice punch.

1½ jiggers Templeton Rye small batch

1 jigger sweet vermouth

1 squirt (about two teaspoons) boozy cherry juice

3 boozy Michigan cherries

whisper of bitters

Put a handful of ice into a cocktail shaker, then add Templeton Rye, sweet vermouth, and boozy cherry juice. Shake well, then pour into a glass. Top with bitters and add boozy cherries. Of course, you can vary the proportions according to your taste.

Boozy Cherry Juice

Stir together equal parts brandy, sweet vermouth, maraschino syrup, and simple syrup. The amount will vary depending on how many cherries you want to steep, but a half cup each should be enough for a several cups of cherries. Add pitted cherries, cover, and refrigerate for four days or up to six weeks.

To make simple syrup, boil equal parts sugar and water until slightly thickened, about five minutes. Remove from heat and cool.

Melissa Dunham of **Grinnell Heritage Farm** farms with her husband, Andrew, on eighty acres that has been in his family for more than 150 years. They have about two hundred CSA members in the summer season and are helpful with preparation tips in their newsletter. Their vegetable offerings range from asparagus, spinach, and radishes in the spring, to potatoes, carrots, and beets later in the season.

Melissa Dunham of Grinnell Heritage Farm

Pinecrest Farm offers a variety of foods, including some particularly delicious Bosc pears. **Anything But Green Gardens** wins the prize for the most breathtaking array of exotic mushrooms I have seen at any farmers' market or grocery store—or anywhere else, for that matter.

Lois Reichert of **Reichert's Dairy Aire** likes to say that goat people have a sense of humor. The first hint is the whimsical name of her business, a playful interpretation of *derrière*, the French word for "behind." Her logo is an illustration of a goat looking over her shoulder, giving you a demure peek at her rear end. And Reichert is clearly in the business for fun and for love, since long days and a lot of dish duty are her lot as the one who both tends the herd and makes the cheese.

Reichert is something of a newbie, but she has already received awards from the American Cheese Society and American Dairy Goat Association since starting in 2007. In addition to the accolades, Reichert appreciates the feedback from the judges; their input notwithstanding, however, Reichert's cheese represents her own taste preference. "I was raised on Velveeta in Kansas," says Reichert, "and I don't like really strong flavors." Thus, her cheese is intentionally on the mild side. She accomplishes this in part by her choice of breed. Like the goats at Prairie Fruits Farm in Illinois, Reichert's herd is composed of long-eared Nubian and almost-no-eared La Mancha milking does. She chose the breeds because their milk has gentler flavor, as opposed to the milk of Topenberg and Alpines, for example, which have a "goatier" taste, she says.

Reichert makes three kinds of cheese: chèvre, a soft fresh cheese; feta, a saltier version made in the Greek style; and her signature Robiola di mi Nonna, a Piedmontese-style aged cheese

Lois Reichert of Reichert's Dairy Aire, with her granddaughter Chelsey Bagley

with a more forward flavor. Her feta is dry salted because she did not like what the traditional method of brining did to the texture of the cheese. Some of her cheeses are embellished with fresh herbs—first chive blossoms in the spring and then basil in the heat of summer, giving her a chance to educate people about seasonality. In all, she has twenty goats, including "the boys," and has set a goal to have twenty pounds of milk per day for cheese she sells at the Des Moines Market, as well as at local stores and through a Chicago distributor. "Goats first" is Reichert's mantra for her focus on managing the health of the herd. Her goats eat their alfalfa off the ground because goats have little resistance to parasites they might ingest while dining on the ground. Reichert spends $6 a bale on quality alfalfa, a hefty price for animal feed. Kids are bottle fed with pasteurized milk. "I want my kids to have mama's milk," said Reichert, "but I find pasteurized milk contributes to a healthier herd."

Reichart made the decision to not become certified organic despite adhering to most organic practices. Under organic standards, milk from any goat that has been given antibiotics could not be included in organic cheese. This restriction is meant to address the industrial practice of administering antibiotics to healthy animals as a precautionary measure. But for Reichert, it means that an animal would have to be discarded if she had been ill or had a difficult kidding and needed a little medicine to recover. Her goats get access to fresh pasture and brush, and the manure goes to compost at neighboring Blue Gate Farm, where it becomes fertilizer. The whey goes to another neighboring farm to feed hogs.

Moving to the south side of Court Avenue we come to **Frisian Farms**, which sells Gouda and only Gouda—young, aged, smoked, and sometimes flavored with Italian herbs or cumin. And Frisian Farms Gouda is pretty delicious throughout its life cycle. Fruity and tangy at a youthful four months, it mellows to honey and butterscotch after two years.

Gouda takes its name from the Dutch city outside Rotterdam famous for it cheese, but some of the wax-encased cheese that came from across the Atlantic fell below expectations. Brothers Jason and Mike Bandstra, who come from Dutch roots and grew up on a dairy farm in Des Moines, knew they could do better with a farmstead Gouda using milk from their own cows. Jason launched their initiative in 2004 with ten Holstein calves and began milking cows in 2005—this, on top of farming grain and working with the international seed company Pioneer HiBred. Today they have eighty milking cows and produce about twelve hundred pounds of Gouda each week. The Bandstras created their own recipe in consultation with a Dutch cheese-maker; now Mike is the primary cheesemaker, and Jason tends and milks the herd.

Mike Bandra of Frisian Farms

The first year they entered the Des Moines Market, 2008, market sales accounted for 50 percent of their total sales. A few years later it is closer to 25 to 30 percent, but that figure changed primarily because their overall production increased. Nevertheless, connecting with their patrons made it all worthwhile. "At 4:30 in the morning I was wondering why I wanted to do this, but every Saturday afternoon I was glad I did," says Mike Bandstra. "We'd start to see the same people coming back every week, and I was surprised at how fun it was to see everyone and get their feedback."

After their success at the Des Moines Market, Bandstra decided to experiment with other markets. The Iowa City Market proved to be a keeper, but another market they tried was disappointing. "We track toothpicks to determine how many samples we distributed; at that market, we used twice the amount of toothpicks and sold half as much cheese," Bandstra says. Frisian Farms is situated in Oskaloosa, snuggled next to the historic Dutch community of Pella. Jason's wife, Valerie, operates the Cheese Maker's Inn in the original farmhouse.

Farm Crawl Illustrates Home Field Advantage

The farmers behind Coyote Run, Blue Gate, and Reichert's Dairy Aire are not just neighbors at the Des Moines market—they are neighbors in farming as well. Back in 2007 Sean Skeehan and Jill Beebout of Blue Gate came up with an idea of a farm crawl, inspired by an art crawl in their former town of Houston, Arizona. Their farm was up and running, and they wanted to have more of a connection with their community, and the neighboring farms were game to welcome visitors. They banded together with Coyote Run Farm, Reichert's Dairy Aire, Schneider Orchards, White Breast Pottery and Weaving, Dan D Farms, and Pierce's Pumpkin Patch. The first year a couple hundred visitors made the trek; in 2010 the designated welcome "clicker" at Blue Gate counted more than thirteen hundred. People can visit all the farms or just a few on the thirty-seven-mile route, and it is a doable day trip only forty-five minutes southwest of Des Moines.

Madison County Farmers' Market

Founded 1993

25+ vendors

Saturdays, May through October

Madison County Courthouse Square, John Wayne Drive and Jefferson Street, Winterset

Winterset in Madison County is not only the birthplace of John Wayne and the setting for the novel and film "The Bridges of Madison County." It is also the setting for a charming farmers' market outside the limestone courthouse that dates to 1876. **Randol Honey** is a must-stop for regulars, and **Hensley's Farm** serves up delicious vegetables, as does **Mary Huss**, **Country Lane Gardens**, and **Bridgewater Farm**. **Burr Oak Farms** is known for its fruit and preserves. **Grandma's Kitchen**, **Vella Beebe**, and **Ruby Adams** bake the goodies.

Boone Farmers' Market

Rinehart Family Farm sells vegetables and honey, and **Cliff Dodd** sells an array of vegetables. **Storybook Orchard** is known for peaches, plums, and berries. **Avenelle and Pat** are known for their baked goods, as is **Bev's Little Bakery**.

12 vendors

Thursdays, June through October

1815 South Story Street, Boone

Council Bluffs Main Street Farmers' Market

Wild Rose Farm and Apiary brings eggs and chicken from lovingly raised poultry breeds Buff Brahma and Barred Plymouth Rock, along with a number of herbs, vegetables, and honey products. **Honey Creek Creamery** sells goat cheese made only ten miles away in the Loess Hills area. Stop by **Our Daily Bread** and **Jody's Natural Kitchen** for baked goods. **Kelly's Berry Best Pies** is the place for dessert.

20 vendors

Thursdays, May through September

Ninth Avenue and South Main Street, Council Bluffs

Sioux City Farmers' Market

On the western border of Iowa along the Missouri River, the Sioux City Farmers' Market offers fresh vegetables and fruit from **D&V Produce**, **Evergreen Farm**, **Wolff Farms**, **Sherer Country Gardens**, **Family Farms Produce**, and **Castle Creek Family Farm**. **Dakota Harvest Farm** sells beef and lamb. Pick up baked goods and bread from **Wheeler Bread**, **Vertigre Bakery**, and **Esmerelda's Bread Basket**. For a hearty start to your shopping, stop by **Real Food** for an omelet cooked to order by Chef Paul Seaman. Pick up worm castings for your garden at **Worm Works Organic Fertilizer**. **Pureside Organics** sells cooking oil made within a hundred miles of the market.

60+ vendors

Wednesdays and Saturdays, May through October

Triview Avenue and Pearl Street, Sioux City

Seed Savers Exchange Preserves Biodiversity

The Seed Savers Exchange was established in 1975 to save and share heirloom seeds. It is headquartered in Decorah, Iowa, on an 890-acre farm, and members are credited with sharing one million samples of rare garden seeds so far. The yearly Seed Savers conference and camp-out draws people from around the world, and while in Iowa, visitors can visit the intimate Winneshiek Farmers' Market.

Winneshiek Farmers' Market

40 vendors

Wednesdays and Saturdays, May through October

Across from City Hall, 400 Claiborne Drive, Decorah

Because the venerated Seed Savers is located outside Decorah, one would expect a vibrant market in its home county of Winneshiek. **Canoe Creek Produce** offers eggs, vegetables, fruit, and meat. **Patchwork Green Farm** grows more than two hundred varieties of vegetables atop a ridge overlooking the Canoe Creek valley. **Yellow River Dairy** produces farmstead goat cheese made by Patricia and Timothy Lund using milk from Saanen, Alpine, and Toggenburg goats. **Given Gardens** is an intimate, five-acre organic farm; owners Nathan and Sarah Wicks are graduates of the Farm Beginnings program offered by the Land Stewardship Project in Minnesota. More vendors include **Kymar Acres** for produce, **G It's Fresh** for organic vegetables, and **Peake Orchards** for fruit.

Dubuque Farmers' Market

Dubuque City Hall anchors its farmers' market, which has been in the city's Upper Main district since 1845, staking a claim as Iowa's oldest open-air market. Here you will find **Hammerand Farm** for certified organic eggs and vegetables, **Johnson Honey Farm**, and **Kruse Farms** for produce, dried fruit, and herbs. Get your beef from **Galena Beef**, **Heritage Beef**, **Black Angus Acres**, and **Life is Good Beef**. **Paris sur Platte** grows garlic, potatoes and other vegetables. Pies and other treats come from Bev Carl, **Fairy Tale Sweets**, and Linda Merfield. **Ambleside Farm** offers seasonal organic vegetables, homemade pasta, and handcrafted soap.

Founded 1845

150+ vendors

Saturdays, May through October

Iowa Street between 13th and 11th Streets, Dubuque

Davenport Freight House Farmers' Market

Situated along the scenic Mississippi River outside the historic Freight House, the market hums on Saturday mornings with shoppers looking for vegetables and fruits from **Country Corner Farm** and **Farmer Ken's Produce**. Meats come from **Sawyer Beef**, **Geest Farms**, **Grossman's Meats**, and **C/W Livestock** bison farm. Furry friends never go neglected with food from **Four Feet Treats** and **Freddie's Fritters Dog Bakery**. **Crandall Farms** sells honey, and **Barb's Pantry** features dozens of preserves. The building itself is evolving into a local food hub with the help of the Davenport government.

80+ vendors

Saturdays, May through October

421 West River Drive, Davenport

Leopold Center for Sustainable Agriculture

Rich Pirog is a legend in local food systems. And his employer, the Leopold Center for Sustainable Agriculture, is one of those organizations that is world famous in agriculture circles—and not very well known to the average eater.

A visit to Ames, about thirty miles straight north of Des Moines—gives a hint about the work going into remaking our food system into one that is more focused on building community. Pirog is a veritable font of farmers' market facts: he knows, for example, that farmers' markets in Iowa account for $20.8 million in annual economic activity and generate 325 jobs. In 2004 more than fifty-five thousand citizens went to at least one farmers' market.

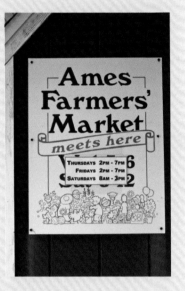

In the introduction to this book, I stated that, on average, food travels fifteen hundred miles to get to the grocery store: Rich Pirog and his team calculated that fact. But even with all this discussion of food miles, Pirog believes it is not about the miles, it is about the relationships. "When people know the person who grows their food, they eat better, and the economy benefits," he says.

And Pirog knows what he is talking about, because he has researched all sorts of things that point to how local foods can strengthen economies, including foods that have a sense of place, like Maytag Blue Cheese, aged in caves near Newton since 1941, or Muscatine melons, a muskmelon that grows well in the sandy soil near the Mississippi River in Muscatine County.

But Pirog says his flagship project was his last one, which started with another statistic: only 14 percent of the $8 billion that Iowans spend on food is grown in Iowa. The Iowa Senate Agriculture Committee asked the Leopold Center to study this issue. In a massive undertaking where more than one thousand people contributed, representing 95 of Iowa's 99 counties, the Leopold Center made recommendations to the legislature in January 2011. Within a month, of all the recommendations that did not require funding measures had already been implemented, such as adding a small farmer to an inspection-and-appeals task force.

One good-news factor is that Iowa has not lost its small meat infrastructure the way other states have. In studies of small-capacity meat processing facilities, ideal for servicing small, organic, pasture-based organizations, researchers determined they can increase profits merely by changing their scheduling.

And the butcher is coming back. "Back in the 1950s and '60s a butcher was a highly skilled wage earner, and often unionized," says Pirog. "Today each worker on the assembly line makes one cut." Now a meat-cutting program is training people to be butchers again.

Pirog announced in early 2011 that he would be moving to Michigan State University to do similar work, after more than twenty years in Iowa. Fred Kirschenmann, the senior fellow at the Leopold Center, is also board president of Stone Barnes Center for Food and Agriculture in New York and heads the Kirschenmann Family Farms, a 3,500-acre certified organic wheat farm in North Dakota. Kirschenmann will continue to carry the torch for local food in Iowa and beyond.

Iowa City Farmers' Market

This market is the only one I found in a parking ramp. Its unusual setting has the advantage of being completely covered, making it convenient for rainy days, and if you squint, you can imagine that you are winding your way around the wide inclines at the Guggenheim in New York. In fact, so much of the food can pass for art.

"When you buy at the market, you get food that actually feeds you, rather than food that just fills you up," says David Miller of **Pure Prairie Gardens** near Mt. Vernon. "If it has flavor; it has the proper nutrition." Shoppers can find everything from fresh pasta to bison. Seek out **Salt Fork Farms** for chicken and eggs, **Brick Arch Winery**, Kate Edwards and **Morgan Creek Market** for fruits and vegetables, and **Bloomin' Prairie Bison** for meat.

Founded 1973

55 vendors

Saturdays, May through October

Across from City Hall, 401 East Washington Street, Iowa City

Iowa Sweet Corn Relish

Kurt Michael Friese, Devotay

Chef Kurt Michael Friese owns Devotay restaurant in Iowa City with his wife, Kim McWane Friese. He is also a writer, publisher of Edible Iowa River Valley, and a governor of Slow Food. He showcases fresh Iowa vegetables, which he buys from Oak Hill Acres, Grinnell Heritage Farm, Adelyn's Organic Garden, and Echollective. His sweet corn relish feeds a crowd at a picnic.

MAKES EIGHT TO TEN CUPS

4 to 6 ears of sweet corn, grilled, then kernels cut from the cob

1 large cucumber, peeled, seeded, and diced

1 large yellow onion, peeled and diced

1 small sweet red bell pepper, seeded and diced

1 small sweet green bell pepper, seeded and diced

2 plum or Roma tomatoes, seeded and diced small

1 fresh hot serrano chili pepper (or to taste), seeded and minced

1½ cups apple cider vinegar (5 percent acidity)

½ cup sugar

2 tablespoons kosher salt

½ teaspoon black pepper

½ teaspoon turmeric

2 teaspoons mustard seed, toasted

½ teaspoon cumin seed, toasted and ground

Toss corn kernels with diced cucumber, onion, peppers, tomatoes, and chili in a large bowl. In a separate bowl, whisk vinegar with sugar, salt, pepper, turmeric, mustard seed, and cumin seed. Pour over vegetables, stir to combine, then refrigerate one hour or as long as overnight. Serve with grilled meats or barbecue.

Step dancers at Mill City Farmers' Market, Minneapolis

Minnesota

Residents of warmer climates may expect little variety from Minnesota, but quite the opposite is true. Minnesota farmers offer a wide diversity of foods to sell at the farmers' markets, including unexpected items like wild rice, house-milled flour, and pasture-raised bison. Farmers' markets have been part of Minnesota life since settlement days—St. Paul's city charter provided for a farmers' market in 1854. And Minnesota is the home to the Honeycrisp apple, one of the greatest farmers' market success stories.

The locations of many Minnesota markets illustrate how settlements, and later cities, grew up near water. Many markets are held in town centers overlooking rivers or lakes. One of our nation's major waterways, the Mississippi River, originates at Lake Itasca in Minnesota and meanders its way through the Twin Cities before becoming the wide, imposing presence made famous by Mark Twain. It is along this river that we find one of the Twin Cities' most significant markets, and an important part of the region's history.

Mill City Farmers' Market

Founded 2006

70+ vendors

Saturdays, May through
October

704 South Second Street
at Mill City Museum,
Minneapolis

The Mill City Farmers' Market puts forward a striking presence on a cloudless, windswept, autumn day and seems to be the quintessential Minneapolis experience. The location itself makes it an attractive destination, situated a block from the Mississippi River and tucked into the Mill City Museum and across from the impressive marble Arlo Guthrie Theater. The market starts under cover, where in the past train cars would pull in to load up on flour. Tents spill out into the open air. Step dancers perform in full lumberjack regalia. A mother-and-daughter pair of goats are at the ready to meet children—and people like me who like goats. The cooking demonstration station had a crowd of about one hundred, and not only for when the cook was handing out the samples.

The 1880 mill—now a museum—heralded five decades of dominance in the milling industry, using water power from the St. Anthony Falls. Grain arrived from the Great Plains, and the Washburn A mill alone made enough flour for 12 million loaves of bread a day. But its technology became obsolete, and the mill closed in 1965 when milling moved away from water power. The building was almost destroyed by fire in 1991. The operation became part of what is now General Mills, still located in the Twin Cities and still making the most widely available brands of flour, Gold Medal and Pillsbury. The ruins were shored up by the Minneapolis Community Development Agency then turned over to the Minnesota Historical Society to develop a museum at the site.

Although the museum is a fantastic example of creative reuse, and it certainly pays homage to the city's heritage as a milling powerhouse, one cannot help but feel uncomfortable to see the ruins of the mills. At one time several flour companies operated in Minneapolis. But, as with so many indications of progress, it stands as a stern reminder of how time marches on and how consolidated

Facing page: The ruins of the 1880 mill, now a museum

our food systems have become, making markets more important to balance things out.

The Mill City Market applies a wider interpretation of what is considered local, expanding to include what might be called handcrafted food, or hand-caught food, in the case of a fisherman who sells Alaska salmon that he has fished from his own boat, frozen, and brought back. And there is a purveyor who sells coffee from his family's plantation in Guatemala.

The market was founded by Brenda Langton, a salt-of-the-earth chef who founded Café Brenda in the late 1970s to serve vegetarian fare featuring local growers, back when local food was considered a fringe hippie movement rather than a way to enjoy the taste of the soil and a connection to neighbors.

Langton was buying from local growers long before this boom time when farmers became the new rock stars of the food world, first at

Café Brenda and later at Spoonriver, right next door to the market. The Mill City Farmers' Market is a natural extension of her devotion to farmers, and likely a way to keep a few in business.

She laments the ongoing discussion about price and cringes at the prickly comments that Mill City is more expensive than other farmers' markets. "We have more organic growers and more niche producers," she says. It does stand to reason that a few pricier standout products would overshadow the reasonably priced vegetables that are widely available. The key is to educate eaters about the value-added nature of some crops as they become available locally at any given market. She speaks of watching vendors "grow up and get better" as they refine their offering.

"Thirty years ago I had farmers deliver vegetables to my restaurant, and I jumped into organizing a market with very little knowledge," she says. Her inexperience does not show, and the market seems to have hit a stride. And now Langton is also a vendor, with a crepe stand serving crepes stuffed with fillings like quork, a sort of crème fraiche made with Amish milk, plus ham and cheese, and a handcrafted chocolate and peanut butter spread.

Farmers at the Mill City Market

» Although most markets offer locally roasted coffee, at this market a local, Carlos Palacios of **Café Palmira**, serves coffee grown on his family's farm in Guatemala. He met his American wife when she was in the Peace Corps stationed in Guatemala. When they settled in the Twin Cities, they would return from visits home with a suitcase full of coffee beans.

Their farming arrangement is symbiotic. About fifteen men work with the Palacios family on the 110-acre farm, and the family loans them acreage not planted with coffee trees for their own use to grown corn and beans to feed their families. Palacios volunteers that although the farm is not certified fair trade, it goes one better because of the close relationship between the family, the workers, and his operation in the United States.

His farm has been in the family for four generations, and their coffee is shade grown at an altitude of eighteen hundred meters. Palacios still travels there every year to help with the harvest, mostly January through March. He now imports a container's worth—forty thousand pounds of fresh green coffee beans, called cherries—and has them roasted at the Bull Run Roasting Company in Minneapolis.

Carlos Palacios sells coffee from his family's farm in Guatemala

» Laura Frerichs of **Loon Organics**, who farms with her husband, Adam Cullip, is one of the young, optimistic farmers making a change in the face of farming. She reflects on the romance of the Mill City Market, talking about the quiet, early-morning setup, then the flurry of activity as shoppers pack the market, "then empty," followed by packing up and returning home.

She brings a philosophy of deep connection to the land. She and her husband came up with the name of their farm while camping in northern Minnesota near the Boundary Waters, a region of wilderness near the Canadian border, where they heard loons calling. "I fell in love with their beautiful and eerie call," she says. "We enjoyed being in nature and with the loons." She adds that the farm's name is a play on words, grinning that anyone would be loony to start a vegetable farm. They acquired their farm from another farming couple making a lifestyle change. They farm on

*Laura Frerichs and Adam Cullip of
Loon Organics*

forty organic acres, of which half is appropriate for cultivation, or "tillable," as Frerichs says.

Frerichs's passion is the Jimmy Nardello Sweet Italian Frying Pepper. She describes it as looking like a cayenne pepper, but not hot, with a thin skin that makes it great for frying. She has been selling plants in the spring for five years. She is surprised by the popularity of what she calls "stalwarts": for example, golden and chiogga beets, Brussels sprouts, different colored carrots, and cauliflower.

» When Matt Oxford of **Wild Run Salmon** chucked his career in finance to move to Alaska, he did not imagine he would be back in the Twin Cities. But Wild Run Salmon allows him to fish part of the year in Alaska and then return to spend time with his children in Minneapolis and bring wild-caught salmon to an eager audience. His business represents how the Mill City Market interprets "local" with a broad brush, opening up to vendors who bring a sustainable philosophy to their businesses and offer choices to market shoppers.

"When I was running a seafood restaurant in Homer, Alaska, I was cashing all these checks from crab fishers. When I saw the amount of the checks, I said to myself 'I should start crabbing.' That was in 1989," says Oxford. He has been selling salmon since 2005 or so, setting out on his fishing vessel, the Blue Ox, during wild salmon season, which runs in May. "It supports my fishing habit to sell here," he says. The best thing for his customers is that they know exactly where the fish comes from and how it was caught. This is in contrast with an experience he had buying fish in a holistically-focused supermarket known for its quality food. "The guy behind the fish counter told me the wild-caught salmon was from a certain river in Alaska. I knew the fishing season for that river didn't start for months," he says. He added that he was not implying

Matt Oxford of Wild Run Salmon

the retailer was being intentionally deceptive, but that it is difficult to be accurate when the salesperson is that far removed from the fish.

》 Alaskan salmon is not the only kind of fish available at Mill City. Northern states are an ideal setting for aquaculture because the chilly weather makes it easier to maintain a cool temperature all year round, and **Star Prairie Trout Farm** has capitalized on this benefit by raising trout. The cool temperatures mean the fish take longer to mature, giving them firmer flesh and more vibrant flavor than fish raised in a more concentrated industrial facility.

》 Paul Red Elk of **Northern Lakes Wild Rice** harvests rice using an ancient Native American method of a two-person canoe and a couple of sticks. One person pushes the canoe with a long pole, something like a Venetian gondolier. The second person bends the rice stalks and gently strokes them with a stick, ensuring that only ripe grains fall into the canoe, leaving the remaining grains to harvest later in the season or to self-seed for next year. The seeds are roasted, or parched, to remove moisture, then hulled to remove the sheath and expose the seed. Finally, they are winnowed to separate the seeds from the hull in an authentic process that has been in use for centuries. Minnesota's Department of Natural Resources has identified seven hundred lakes with wild rice.

Michael Noreen
of Burning River Farm

》 Jeffrey Nistler of **Nistler Farms** is known to say, "Sweet corn doesn't end: eventually we give up." His sweet corn is known to last well into October, if the frost holds off. Nistler also sells honey, watermelon, and squash.

》 **Sunshine Harvest Farm** sells chemical-free beef, pork, lamb, chicken, and eggs. **Burning River** grows fifty varieties of vegetables and fruit with a Certified Naturally Grown label. **Schultz Farm** offers rhubarb and jams. **Star Thrower Farm** sells a diverse mix, including yarn, pelts, sheep's milk cheeses, and soap. **Singing Hills Goat Dairy** sells goat's milk cheese. **Star Prairie Trout Farm**, **Riverbend Farm**, **Mai and Yia Thao**, and **Hidden Stream Farm** also sell at Mill City, among many, many others. You can find anything you could possibly want to eat here.

Shoppers won't go away hungry, either. **Aunt Else's Aebleskiver** serves up spherical pancakes, sometimes with an apple slice tucked inside. The Scandinavian delicacy is "griddled" in a special cast iron pan with golfball-sized divots. **Bramblewood Cottage** sells Scottish-inspired cookies and treats. **Heath Glen's Farm and Kitchen** serves up fruit preserves, syrups, and chutneys, and **Sonny's Ice Cream** sells small-batch seasonal creamy goodness. Be sure to stop by **Prairie Hollow** or **Solomon** for a crusty loaf. **Sunrise Flour Mill** sells flour if you would prefer to bake your bread at home. **Ames Farm** is your source for raw honey.

St. Paul Farmers' Market

Founded 1853; present location since 1982

100+ vendors

Saturdays and Sundays, May through November; Saturdays, December through April

290 East Fifth Street, St. Paul

Across the river the St. Paul Market has a different vibe, one that seems more utilitarian and with a much longer pedigree than the newer market at Mill City. The market dates to the city's early days, and there is a permanent structure where producers pull up and sell from the backs of their trucks. From the air the market structure looks like a giant extended "E" with three long aisles extending from the base. The location harkens back to when market shopping was less entertaining, with no tony theaters, no step dancers or petting goats. The food, though, is exceptional.

The **Gilbertsons Farms** are Food Alliance certified and have a diversified farm with about three hundred acres of vegetables. The folks at **North Tomah Cranberries** trekked over the St. Croix River from Wisconsin. **Whole Grain Milling Company** is a rare, local company that carries on the area's milling tradition.

Der Thao of **Der's Floral** is a Hmong vendor who sells her floral creations next to her parents, Cha and Ma, who have been selling vegetables in St. Paul for more than twenty-five years, ever since they were new immigrants in this country. Shoppers go to **Bar 5** and **Prairie**

Der Thao and her parents

Pride Farm for pork, Callister Farms for poultry, and Farm On Wheels for lamb and beef. Start your stroll with a stop at Golden's Guiltless Bagels and stop by Lengsfeld Organic Gardens and Adelmann's Farm Market for vegetables.

Stillwater Farmers' Market

Farther east, along the St. Croix River that divides Minnesota and Wisconsin, lies Stillwater, a charming town that has made the transition from industry to tourism. Strolling the streets, I found the charming Chestnut Street Books, a cooking school, and a co-op featuring all kinds of local foods.

The farmers' market is at the foot of the courthouse. L. R. "Dick" Schwartz, a robust, eighty-four-year old, says "What do I need a business card for? I'm a farmer," dismissing the idea that a book author might want to call for an interview. While some farms have web sites and

18 vendors

Saturdays, June through October

Third and Pine Streets, across from historic courthouse, Stillwater

Dick Schwartz sells apples at the Stillwater Farmers' Market

Facebook fan pages and twitter feeds, Schwartz embraces the old-fashioned approach of showing up and letting the fruit speak for itself. But his approach to his Honeycrisp apples is a little different. Some Honeycrisps are large, the size of a child's head in some cases. Schwartz thins less, leaving more apples on the tree, which causes the apples to be smaller.

Stop by **Wittig Farms** for free-range chickens. **Guy Brown** is known as the baked potato man with spuds bigger than his hand. **Nature's Nectar** sells an array of honey and beeswax products. The **White Bear Soap Company** sells dozens of handmade soaps. Score maple syrup from **Weiss Woods** of Plum Creek, and be sure to pick up baked goods from Heather Peterson at **Bread Art**. Betty Van Someren of **Someren Gardens** is your source for vegetables, and she also takes canning and freezing orders.

Farm Beginnings Began in Minnesota

Farm Beginnings is the flagship program of the Land Stewardship Project, and that is no small feat, given that this member organization has a vast array of organizing, education, and activist initiatives. Farm Beginnings supports the Land Stewardship Project's mission of supporting sustainable agriculture and communities. It has three offices in Minnesota to cover the greater Twin Cities, the Driftless region, and the prairie to the west.

Like the Grow Your Farm program in Missouri, which Farm Beginnings inspired, the training focuses on hands-in-the-earth knowledge of getting started in farming. Students visit farms and learn from farmers and bankers who visit the classroom. The Farm Beginnings program has grown to other states, including Illinois and New York, as well as North Dakota and South Dakota.

Father of the Famed Honeycrisp

If apples were rock stars, then the Honeycrisp is Bono. I draw the connection to the lead singer of the Irish group U2 because both are wildly popular, with substance and longevity to back them up. And both come from somewhat humble beginnings, but today both are instantly recognizable.

A blogger named Fruitslinger, who writes anonymously about working for an orchard at a farmers' market, talks about how the Honeycrisps are the first to be sold out and that patrons insist that he choose which of the other apples is closest to the Honeycrisp. A Michigan U-pick orchard reports a line out on the state highway on the first day the Honeycrisp trees are ready. Moms report that their adult children bemoan "deprived" childhoods because they were never fed Honeycrisp apples.

The University of Minnesota developed the Honeycrisp apple, one that has captured the imagination of an eager public and taken farmers' markets by storm. Almost fifty years after its genesis, the Honeycrisp is an "overnight" success, when one considers that many heirloom apples are still orchard favorites, like the McIntosh, which dates to 1798 Ontario, Canada; the Northern Spy from 1800s New York; and Golden Grimes from West Virginia in 1832.

It is here, at the University of Minnesota, where David Bedford is an apple whisperer. In the course of his job, Bedford may walk up to seven miles a day tasting apples. And after thirty years, he does not seem to be slowing down. The day I spoke with David Bedford was a good one. He had given out a number, MN 2072. This red-letter moment requires a little perspective.

The university has about twenty thousand apple trees. Walking through the orchard, Bedford tastes up to six hundred apples a day, every weekday, all through the growing season. This means that he tastes apples from every tree. While tasting and walking, he notes an apple's texture, flavor, and appearance. If it passes muster, it gets a number. Out of 600 apples a day from 20,000 trees a year, about ten to fifteen apples get numbers annually: that is a lot of tasting and tossing. The Honeycrisp received a number back in the late 1960s. Then it went through a discovery period where it was evaluated for factors such as disease resistance. The Honeycrisp does not come from a pedigree in the way a heritage chicken might. After genetic testing, Bedford's team has identified only one parent, the Keepsake, released by the university in 1978. Keepsake is a late-season apple, and sister to the Sweet 16, a more recent release.

The creation of a blockbuster apple is a long process. First, breeders cross two apple trees, then raise them until they bear fruit, then evaluate. If one is good enough to deserve a number, the next step is ten to twenty years of testing. The Honeycrisp was first bred in 1960 but was not released until 1991. Once it is released, the apple stays on patent for fifteen years, meaning growers need to pay one dollar per bushel of apples to the university until the variety rotates off patent; this puts a little pressure on breeders to replace that income by releasing new apples. Does Bedford believe either the SweeTango or Sweet 16 will match the excitement of the Honeycrisp?

"The Honeycrisp is kind of like winning the lottery," he says. And it really is like a lottery. One imagines that apple breeding might be like animal breeding, where award-winning parents are likely to result in superior children. In this case, Bedford's team did DNA testing on the Honeycrisp and were able to identify only one grandparent, meaning that the other three ancestors were only numbered apples which did not grow up to be released. Bedford has no regrets about the possibilities of the lost grandparents. "We always move forward," he says.

But one wonders about the tenuous nature of this breeding program. If the next person who follows in Bedford's footsteps does not have the same palate and attuned tastebuds, might we miss out on the next rock-star apple? The quest for the next "big" apple is complicated by consumer preferences. Bedford explains that Americans seem to be drawn to really red apples, which is why the Red Delicious came to be the lunchbox apple of the nation. Bedford's childhood memories include always being stuck with his Red Delicious apple. "I could never trade away a Red Delicious apple," says Bedford. "No one wanted it." When he grew up, he concluded that it lacks texture and has an unbalanced flavor. "It probably tasted different when it was first released, but apples change over time." He speculates that most good apples may be ruined by their own popularity.

He might instead have become the apple whisperer simply by having his own focus group every weekend at the farmers' market. "I had a small orchard and learned firsthand that farmers' market shoppers are a discriminating crowd," he says. Bedford cites a mystery apple that was russet and none too beautiful. But it was delicious. And people kept coming back asking for the "ugly apple," rejecting the prettier sisters without a second glance. That was when Bedford realized that looks are a distant third in the apple world, behind texture and flavor, which the nonred apple delivered in spades. That apple was the Chestnut Crab, which I found at a Minnesota market, still selling well. It outsold Bedford's pretty red apples at a ratio of five to one.

Bedford describes apple flavors in a way one typically associates with sophisticated wine tasters. He says the Sweet 16 has hints of cherry lifesaver and anise, and that the Keepsake has the flavor of raw sugar cane.

The vagaries of apple breeding serve up continual surprise. A large-fruited parent crossed with a small-fruited one does not always result in a medium-sized apple. The Honeycrisp is an example of how the un-pedigreed orphan grew up to become president. But the numbered tree from today is one of her offspring, indicating the possibility of a Honeycrisp dynasty someday—which is saying something, since about 90 percent of apples are discarded.

Bedford credits New Zealand exporters of the Granny Smith apple with breaking the stranglehold of the Red Delicious on the American palate. Once people realized that apples could come in many colors, they started to taste and experiment. Another reason all-red apples may not be the tastiest is that it is more difficult to see if it is ripe. A two-tone apple gives more hints that it is ready for eating,

David Bedford sold Chestnut Crab apples on his way to working with the University of Minnesota apple program

indicating to orchard workers that they can get out the refractometer to test the sugar content. Red apples turn deep red about three weeks before they are ripe, meaning that they can end up in a crate before any flavor has developed.

Bedford has good news for amateur orchardists—the Honeycrisp makes a good backyard apple because it is resistant to disease and is easy to grow. Now I just have to wait eight years or so for the fruit.

Red Wing Farmers' Market

Founded 2007

40+ vendors

Daily, April through October

Train Depot, 212–290 Levee Street, Red Wing

About forty-five miles southeast of St. Paul is Red Wing, a charming, historic town on the Mississippi River, home to the sturdy Red Wing Shoes favored by many farmers. Red Wing was once the world's primary wheat market and home to three stoneware companies. And although its current iteration has been in place for only a few years, its farmers' market dates back about fifty years. At this farmers' market you can get your veg on with **Thurston Hill Produce**, **Bao and Shua Garden**, **Bystrom Produce**, **LC Vegetable Garden**, and **Leng Gardens**. **Hartland Prairie Farm** offers native flowers and grasses. Buy honey from **River Road Honey Farm**, organic heirloom vegetables and fruit from **Overlander Organics**, and organic soaps and lotions from **Shady Lane Farm**. Kick off the season with strawberries from **Bushel and Peck** and rhubarb from **Dennis's Produce**; also, try some handmade German-style sausage from **Comfort Food**. Pick up baked goods at **Dana's Bread**, **Grateful Bread**, or **B.E. Gluten Free**. **Ewes Rule Farm** features an array of lamb products and sheep cheeses.

St. Joseph Farmers' Market

Founded 2000

28 vendors

Fridays, May through October

Under the city water tower, four blocks north of Highway 75 on County Road 2, St. Joseph

The Lake Wobegon Regional Trail is a bike and hike trail that traverses the central lakes of Minnesota. Near the beginning of this trail, under the city water tower, we find the St. Joseph Farmers' Market. A majority of foods at the market come from a tight thirty-mile radius. Find **Scenic Waters Wild Rice**, grass-fed beef and pork at **Rolling Hills Traeger Ranch**, and organic milk from **Three Rivers Farm**. **Neumann Farms** offers pork and pies, and **Collegeville Orchards** is known for more than twenty varieties of apples, including State Fair, Redwell, and Prairie Spy. **Cedar Hill Farm** specializes in heirloom fruits and vegetables. Shoppers at **Common Ground Farm** can choose from dozens of vegetables. **Morning Star Farm** serves up artisan cheese made with milk from Brown Swiss pasture-fed cows. **Produce Acres** kicks off the season with asparagus, rhubarb, and berries, and continues the season through to pumpkins and gourds.

Grand Rapids Farmers' Market

Vendors at the Grand Rapids Market are all based within fifty miles of Grand Rapids, so freshness abounds. Try free-range eggs from **Prairie River Farm**, and beef, pork, and chicken from **Willow Sedge Farm** or **Block's Balsam Lake Farm**. **Great River Gardens** sells plants and produce like asparagus, berries, and tomatoes. Find more vegetables at **River Road Farm**, **Grand Rapids Greenhouse**, **Nordas Acres**, **Schmidt Farm**, and **Clayton's Produce**, known for its tomatoes. **Albin Alto Farm** grows organic garlic, potatoes, and other vegetables. Get honey from **TimberSweet** and **Bar Bell Bee Ranch**. Baked goods come from **Yoder Family Baking Company**.

40 vendors

Mondays, Wednesdays, and Saturdays, May through October

Highway 2 between First Avenue NW and Second Avenue NW, Grand Rapids

Maple Grove Farmers' Market

Trumpeter Swan Farm serves up berries, vegetables, and free-range eggs from their forty-acre farm. **Beck's Greenhouse** offers bedding plants and a vast array of vegetables and melons. **Long Siding Farm** produces USDA organic fruits and vegetables. **Ames Farm** is an apiary and orchard. **Thompson's Hillcrest Orchard** sells raspberries, pumpkins, and apples from eleven hundred trees. **Neumann Farms** sells beef and pork, plus sweet corn, raspberries, and pies. Joyce Neumann is known for her strawberry rhubarb pie. And get maple syrup from **Stanley's Sugarbush**. Maple Grove has a few novel vendors as well: get flax and barley from the aptly named **Flax & Barley** and emu meat and oil products from **Hassu Lintu Emu Ranch**. **Collegeville Artisan Bakery** and **Breadsmith** serve the baked goods.

50+ vendors

Thursdays, June through October

Maple Grove Community Center, 12951 Weaver Lake Road, Maple Grove

Renewing the Countryside with Farmer Speed Dating

Brett Olson of Renewing the Countryside is moving to the farm. He cofounded this nonprofit that champions local eating with his wife, Jan Joannides, as an extension of her thesis about land-use management—that, and a little inspiration from a book they found in the Netherlands by the same name. Renewing the Countryside shares inspiring stories of small farmers and promotes sustainable tourism with an eye toward reinvigorating small-town American. The initiative has a website and Local Food Hero radio program, and it has compiled the luscious *Minnesota Homegrown Cookbook*, filled with recipes and profiles of their local food heroes. I spoke with Olson, whose contagious optimism will refresh many a small town if he has anything to do about it.

"We wanted to find active solutions to help the Main Streets that are falling apart because of a depressed economy and lack of vibrancy," he said. By sharing the stories of people who are doing vibrant things in rural areas, Olson hopes to make connections that help more people succeed. In addition to media vehicles, Renewing the Countryside also goes straight to the people.

"We coordinated more than forty-eight food demonstrations at the Minnesota State Fair," says Olson, reaching more than 350,000 people at the fair. But to my mind, their most compelling program is farmer–chef speed dating.

"We realized that both chefs and farmers are back-of-the-house people," says Olson, meaning that they are used to keeping their heads down and doing the work, not reaching out and making connections. "We set up meetings where farmers and chefs get five minutes together, then rotate," Olson explains. No one has to have a lengthy conversation, but chefs can find the fava beans they are looking for, and farmers can find out how to tweak their crop offerings to boost revenue. While attendance will vary based on an area's population, a Twin Cities gathering drew seventy farmers and thirty restaurants, an outstanding set of connections by any standards, when you consider how long it would take a farmer to visit thirty restaurants one by one. Next on the agenda: match immigrant growers with ethnic restaurants.

Olson and Joannides plan their own countryside escape by transitioning from a house in St. Paul just blocks from restaurants and their co-op grocery store to a forty-acre farm and vineyard in Zumbro Falls, about an hour's drive southeast of the city.

Duluth Farmers' Market

At the western tip of Lake Superior lies Duluth, which has hosted a farmers' market for a century. A long, low-slung red barn has been the market's location since 1953. Here you will find maple syrup from **Spirit Lake**, vegetables at **River's Edge Gardens**, tomatoes and plants from **Shubat's Fruits**. Rounding out the offerings are **Skalko's Honey Bee Farm**, the **Walters Family Miel**, **Mike's Nostalgic Harvest**, **K & Z Farm**, and **Talmadge Farms**. At the end of the season, get a balsam wreath from **Doug and Lois Hoffbauer**.

Founded 1911

12+ vendors

Wednesdays and Saturdays, May through October

14th Avenue E and Third Street, Duluth

Lake Superior Whitefish and Spring Vegetables in Parchment Pouch

Judi Barsness, Chez Jude Restaurant and Wine Bar

Chef Judi Barsness of Chez Jude Restaurant and Wine Bar proves once and for all that anyone can eat locally with a little effort and ingenuity. In Grand Marais, on the north shore of Lake Superior, Barsness has assembled a crew of suppliers such as Harley and Shele Toftey of Dockside Fish Market and Lisa and Eric Klein of Hidden Stream Farm, who provide fresh local ingredients for a season that lasts longer than one might think.

SERVES FOUR

4 each red, Yukon gold, and blue potatoes, skin on, thinly sliced

2 asparagus spears, trimmed and cut into three-inch sections

16 spring ramps or leeks, cut in half lengthwise

12 baby carrots, cut in half lengthwise

24 morel and/or shitake mushrooms, halved or quartered

1 cup butter, melted

½ cup Meyer lemon juice, from one or two lemons

Lemon zest

1 to 2 tablespoons fresh chopped parsley

8 fresh chive stems, chopped

Salt and pepper to taste

Fresh chive stems and flowers for garnish

Cut eight pieces of parchment paper into 8-inch heart shapes and preheat oven to 450 degrees. Stir lemon juice and zest into melted butter and season with salt and pepper.

On the side of each heart-shaped pouch, near to the fold, layer potato slices, using each color, and season with salt and pepper. Top with fish fillet and sprinkle with salt and pepper again. Layer on asparagus, baby carrots and mushrooms; salt and pepper once more. Drizzle with lemon butter. Sprinkle with chopped parsley and chives.

To form the pouch, fold the paper over the fish and vegetables. Beginning at one end, fold and crease the edges together securely so no juices escape and the food steams within the pouch. You will have a small tail of parchment paper: fold that securely under the pouch. Place on a baking sheet and bake until very puffed, about ten to fifteen minutes. Remove from oven and place on a plate. Garnish top of pouch with a crossed stem of chive flowers and fresh chive. Serve with a pair of scissors to open the top.

Variation: as a substitute for whitefish, use Lake Superior lake trout, walleye, wild-caught Alaskan sockeye salmon, or jumbo sea scallops, shrimp, or any favorite fish.

Natural Choice Farmers' Market

My friend and fellow writer Sue Doeden goes to the Natural Choice Farmers' Market in far north Bemidji to get ingredients for her weekly food column in the *Bemidji Pioneer* newspaper. Doeden tells me she visits the market several times a week for heirloom tomatoes, beautiful greens, and beets. Some of her favorite vendors include vegetable purveyors **Dick's Produce**, **Full Moon Farm**, and **Chill Creek Ridge**, which grows organically. **Franklin Gardens** offers vegetables and orchard fruit. **Kroeger & Rixen Farm** is truly diversified, with fruits, vegetables, honey and beeswax, pickles, maple syrup, and jams. **Paradise Valley Buffalo Ranch** sells bison, and **Fair Acres** is the source for chicken and eggs. Shopping—and selling—must be a pleasure in the lovely setting overlooking Lake Bemidji.

Founded 2010

12 vendors

Wednesdays and Saturdays, June through November

200 Paul Bunyon Drive South, across from Paul Bunyon and Babe the Blue Ox, Bemidji

The Dane County Farmers' Market surrounds the Wisconsin state capitol

Wisconsin

By the time our journey leads us to Wisconsin, it is clear that the Midwest has a dynamic local food scene, despite the challenges facing small farms. Every farmers' market has vegetables and fruits; bakeries; often meat, poultry, and eggs; and sometimes locally roasted coffee—each market with its own story and distinctive collection of boosters and curmudgeons.

Wisconsin's distinction is having cheese, and lots of it. The state has more than 1.2 million dairy cows, many of them in small herds grazing on the rolling pasture. More than 90 percent of Wisconsin milk is made into cheese. A lot of it goes on hamburgers at fast food joints, but the specialty cheeses have captured the attention of food enthusiasts around the world.

Wisconsin Cheese by the Numbers

1.265 million dairy cows

1,185 licensed cheesemakers

51 master cheesemakers

600+ varieties, types, and styles of cheese

98 ribbons at the American Cheese Society competition in 2010,
attended by 225 companies in 34 states, plus Canada and Mexico

Dane County Farmers' Market

Since 1972

300+ vendors

Wednesdays and
Saturdays, April through
November

Capitol Square,
downtown Madison

The striking white capitol dome reigns over the weekly
Dane County Farmers' Market, widely considered the
best market in the nation, and not only for its dramatic
presence. The diversity of vendors—cheese, meat, baked
goods, doughnuts, copious varieties of apples—is breathtaking, and it is the only market where I found a vendor
selling hickory nuts. Many vendors are vegetable growers whose names are frequently flagged on restaurant
menus. It is no wonder the market can boast up to
twenty-five thousand shoppers on any given Saturday,
and twice that many on special event days. Shoppers
stroll counterclockwise; don't try to buck tradition by
walking in the opposite direction—you'll end up like a
salmon swimming upstream. Best to cross the street,
double back, and cross back into the market stream.

    The Dane County Farmers' Market hosts a good half-
dozen or more artisan cheesemakers, making it a perfect place for a do-it-yourself cheese tour showcasing
Wisconsin artisans.

There is Willi Lehner of **Bleu Mont**, whose bandaged cheddar was lauded by the Wine Spectator as one of the hundred best cheeses in the world. Lehner is a first-generation American, son of Swiss immigrants who came to Wisconsin in the 1950s with cheesemaking experience and dreams. Lehner buys milk from Mike Gingrich of Uplands Cheese Company. And although Lehner's cheese is sought-after everywhere, it is his cave that is the envy of his fellow cheesemakers.

Willi Lehner of Bleu Mont

While I was visiting various cheesemakers in the area, the first question was "Did you see Willi's cave?" It is a half-round structure made with narrow I-beams and rebar, then buried under six feet of soil. It creates the perfect temperature and does not require heating, cooling, or humidity control. The climate is perfect for aging bandaged cheddar, cheese wrapped in a muslin cloth to age. When the cheese is ready, Lehner peels the "bandage" and tosses it in the compost. His bandaged cheddar and Alpine Renegade cheeses have created substantial buzz among cheese devotees.

Head down the square and meet Brenda Jensen of **Hidden Springs Creamery**, a sheep's milk cheese operation with more than three hundred milking ewes. Jensen

Farmstead cheese: cheese made on the farm where the animal is milked.

Artisan cheese: small-batch, hand-crafted cheese, often with proprietary custom recipes.

Brenda Jensen of Hidden Springs Creamery

supplements her supply with cow's milk from her Amish neighbors to make Meadow Melody, her first mixed-milk cheese. The Driftless region of Wisconsin—the hilly portion of the state not scraped flat by glaciation—is where Brenda Jensen makes her cheese. She farms with draft horses Chief and Beauty.

And I am sure to stop by **Fantome**. A *grande dame* of goat cheese, Anne Topham, is widely considered to be one of the leading goat-cheese makers in the country. The Dane County Market is her bread and butter, and she is here almost every week. If I have not spent my cheese allowance yet, I will stop by **Hook's**, **Brunkow** (for its Avondale Truckle), or **Forgotten Valley**—up to a dozen Wisconsin cheeses in all at the market.

And across Carroll Sreet is **Fromagination**, a cheese emporium with more than forty Wisconsin cheeses, where sampling is abundant and other Wisconsin products line the shelves.

More Farmers at the Dane County Market

>> Bill Weston of **Weston Antique Apple Orchard** did not like farming when he was growing up. "All my friends were off playing video games and I was working in the hot sun and getting poison ivy," he says. But after ten years away from Wisconsin, he returned in 1999 and is now, with his father, Ken Weston, the steward behind Weston Antique Apple Orchards in New Berlin, with panoramic views of Waukesha County about fifteen miles southwest of Milwaukee. Now we can see him every Saturday at Dane County, along with his sister, Genevieve, also a partner in the family business.

It is not a surprise that Weston was drawn back to the farm. The sixteen acres of orchards he works with his father have been in his family for generations. His grandparents Alice and Harvey Weston founded the orchard on a site owned by Alice's father. Alice gets the credit for focusing on unusual varieties. "It's one of my father's proudest accomplishments that this land will never have a subdivision on it," he says. Ken and Genevieve gave eleven acres of the orchard to the town of New Berlin with the stipulation that it remain an orchard, or a "passive park," as Bill explains. They formed a foundation to oversee the stewardship of the land and to generate funding to pay for maintenance. The Westons teach bench grafting classes for people who have their own Johnny Appleseed ambitions.

   Visitors can tour the farm and buy apples from the farmstand every Sunday from Labor Day through Thanksgiving, give or take a few weeks, depending on when the apples are ready. For example, a warm spring means that apples can be two to three weeks early. The busiest

Brother and sister team
Bill and Genevieve Weston

A few heirloom apples cultivated at Weston Antique Apple Orchard

APPLE	ORIGIN	DATE
Cox's Orange Pippin	England	1830
Golden Russet	New York	Prior to 1845
Grimes Golden	West Virginia	1832
Idared	Idaho	1942
Jonathan	New York	Prior to 1826
McIntosh	Ontario, Canada	1798
Northern Spy	New York	1800
Pink Pearl	California	1944
Red Cortland	Geneva, New York	1915
Smokehouse	Pennsylvania	1837
Snow	Canada	Prior to 1824
Summer Rambo (Rambour Franc)	France	1535
Wolf River	Wisconsin	Prior to 1881

days are Historic Day in September and Applefest on the first Sunday in October, with dancing in the orchard barn, a barbershop quartet, hand-cranked ice cream, demonstrations of spinning, blacksmithing, and a parade of vintage tractors led by a color guard.

The Westons grow more than one hundred varieties of apples on their sixteen acres with seven hundred trees. They are the only known farm to grow the Old Church apple, a tart apple thought to originate at the nearby First Free Will Church, founded in the mid-1800s.

The history of fruits is colorful and storied, and none so much as the apple. Some apples that we still eat today, such as the diminutive Lady apple, date back to Roman times. The Summer Rambo has French roots back to 1535 and was introduced to this continent by Swedish immigrant Peter Gunnerson Rambo, who arrived on our shores in 1640 with seeds from his farm. In the early days of our country, Johnny Appleseed, born John Chapman in 1774 in Massachusetts, traveled across Ohio, Indiana, and Illinois starting nursery orchards and selling the saplings to farmers to use for hard cider. The Esopus Spitzenberg dates to the 1790s and was grown by Thomas Jefferson at Monticello.

But the beloved apple—considered the most American of fruits—has experienced a decline in recent generations as large orchards began to focus on fewer and fewer varieties. While thousands of apple varieties exist, only about a dozen or so are available in supermarket produce bins. And the food preservation organization Renewing America's Food Traditions Alliance tells us that Red Delicious apples account for a whopping 41 percent of the apple crop in the United States. Slow Food even declared 2010 the year of the apple as a means to drive awareness of the vast varieties of apples that need to be saved.

» Paul and Louise Maki of **Blue Skies Berry Farm** get two harvests from their red and golden raspberries. They "graduated" to a spot on the square after years selling at the outpost stalls that spill over into the side streets. They farm in Brooklyn, about twenty miles due south of Madison. Paul Maki is the one who gave me the best tip about saving a little cash on some of their jewel-toned fruit.

"If you're making jams or sauces, call ahead and ask for 'seconds' because I only sell perfect berries at the market," he says. "I can save you some less-than-perfect berries if you are going to be smashing them anyway." Maki's only-the-best philosophy illustrates many farmers' commitment to quality.

Paul Maki of Blue Skies Berry Farm

» Josh Engel of **Driftless Organics** may seem like a young whippersnapper—handsome, bearded, and still in his 20s—but he has been farming since age eleven. He and his younger brother Noah, sons of a dairy farmer, began their farming career by growing twenty colorful varieties of potatoes. Some years later Mike Lind joined the mix, and now the trio grows everything from "asparagus to zucchini," essentially anything that will grow in the rich Wisconsin soil.

Perhaps their most unusual crop is sunflowers, used to make edible oil you can buy at their table at the Dane County Market. "We plant the sunflowers like field corn," says Lind. Driftless plants about eighty acres, making it the largest crop on its one-hundred-acre farm. Sunflower seeds go into the ground in the spring and bloom in August. By October they are looking nice and ratty, meaning they are dried out and ready for harvest via combine—again, just like corn—which makes a first pass at separating the seed and blowing off the

Josh Engel of Driftless Organics

chaff. Next is the cleaning process. The farmers use an old 1940s cleaner, a vintage machine that separates the seeds from the chaff. The seeds then get transported to Spooner, Wisconsin, for pressing at one of the few certified organic oil-pressing facilities, about two hundred miles north, within a few miles of the Minnesota border. "We wish it were closer, but there aren't enough pressing facilities anymore," Lind said.

Driftless Organics received a USDA Value-Added Producer Grant (VAPG) for $80,000. This planning grant helps with research and development as well as marketing to develop branding for their sunflower oil. The VAPGs are matching-grant initiatives from the USDA with a simple premise: they help farmers make more money. A dairy farmer can increase revenue tremendously by

Harmony Valley Farm

making cheese rather than selling milk to the co-op. Same with grape growers who make wine, vegetable growers who create a sauce brand, and so on. And sunflower growers who sell their own oil. Because competition is steep, Driftless Organics will need to determine if there is a sufficient demand for organic, small-batch sunflower oil. The commodity sunflower crops in the Dakotas result in commercial oil that is half the price. Nevertheless, there seems to be an eager audience for this oil; they sell at co-ops from Madison to the Twin Cities, and in nearby Viroqua, as well as at the Madison market.

Dale Marsden of Marsden's Pure Honey

» Up the path from Weston is **Snug Haven Farm**, whose spinach is the go-to green in Midwest winters. Bill Warner and Judy Hageman grow ten acres under a hoop house and sell out with each planting. Be sure to check out **Marsden's Pure Honey**—you can't miss Dale Marsden in his bee hat. **Harmony Valley** is known for outstanding vegetables, and you can score unusual meats at **Golden Dreams Ostrich Farm** and **Cherokee Bison Farms**. Find **Hickory Nut Heaven** after their autumn harvest.

Grilled Ribeye with Tomato Salad and Bleu Mont Bandaged Cheddar

Tory Miller, L'Etoile

Chef Tory Miller is carrying the torch lit by Odessa Piper, visionary chef whose famed L'Etoile in Madison put farm-to-table eating on the map in the Midwest. While some say that Odessa Piper is the Alice Waters of the Midwest, others grin and let you know that Alice Waters is the West Coast version of Odessa Piper. Regardless, Chef Miller has big shoes to fill and clearly takes his role seriously. At a dinner he outlines his choice of purveyors and says things like, "I wanted to be sure you had the chance to try the 15-year-old cheddar from Hook's." Incidentally, Hook's also sells at the market.

Grilled Fountain Prairie Farm dry-aged ribeye with Tomato Mountain heirloom tomato salad and shaved Bleu Mont Dairy raw-milk bandaged cheddar

SERVES FOUR

4 ribeye steaks (prefer dry-aged at least 21 days)

1 red onion

Selection of heirloom tomatoes (at least 4 varieties, such as Aunt Ruby's German Green, Cherokee Purple, Jean Flamme, Wapsapinacon Peach, Striped German)

2 tablespoons red wine vinegar

6 tablespoons extra virgin olive oil

6 ounces raw-milk bandaged cheddar cheese

6-8 basil leaves

1 clove garlic

4 sprigs rosemary

4 sprigs parsley (leaves only)

Kosher salt, black pepper

Preheat your grill on high heat. Season the ribeyes with salt and let sit at room temperature for at least thirty minutes, up to one hour. When ready to cook, season both sides with black pepper and place on the hottest part of the grill for 1½ minutes per side, then place on the coolest part of the grill for two minutes per side. Do not turn more than four times.

Place the rosemary sprigs on the grill for five seconds. Put on a large plate or tray. Remove the steaks from the grill and rub all over with the garlic clove. Place each on a sprig of rosemary and drizzle with two ounces of extra virgin olive oil. Let rest fifteen minutes before serving.

While the steak is resting, core and cut the tomatoes into a ½-inch dice. Place into a bowl. Slice the onion as thinly as you can and toss gently with the tomatoes. Add the parsley leaves, red wine vinegar, extra virgin olive oil, and torn basil leaves. Season with kosher salt and black pepper. Place each on a serving plate topped with the tomato salad and liberally shred the cheese over the top.

A Word About Artisan Cheese

Before we move on to other farmers' markets, it is worth talking about how the state's specialty cheese business has taken hold, because Wisconsin has reared its bovine head as the premier cheesemaking state for a reason. First, of course, is the mineral-rich soil, well suited for growing pasture grasses, and the rolling terrain that lends itself to grazing cows.

I talked with cheese expert Jeanne Carpenter of Wisconsin Cheese Originals. So enamored with Wisconsin cheesemakers was Carpenter that she gave up a high-powered job as spokesperson with the Wisconsin Department of Agriculture to focus exclusively on cheese. Now the owner of a public relations firm and the Wisconsin Cheese Originals show, and publisher of the Cheese Underground blog, Carpenter is one of those lucky folks who have married passion with livelihood. She ends of lot of sentences with a hearty giggle, a sort of joyful punctuation mark that makes it clear that she takes delight in her work.

Back when Wisconsin cheese production was on its decline, Carpenter and a small collection of intrepid souls saw a future for specialty cheeses that could wow the nation's palate, even the world's. They committed to regaining Wisconsin's crown as the country's leading cheese producer—not in just tonnage, but in hold-on-to-your-hat, holy-smokes-this-is-good specialty cheese.

Carpenter is a founding member of the Dairy Business Innovation Center (DBIC), a not-for-profit organization created with grant funding. This small, focused team went out to meet with dairy farmers to find out what they needed to thrive. "We sat around a lot of kitchen tables talking about what it would take to help dairy farmers succeed," says Carpenter.

In 2003, the year the DBIC was founded, Wisconsin's cheese empire was in the midst of a long, slow decline, losing one to five cheese plants every year. Since its founding, forty-three new plants have been installed across the state and sixty-five new products introduced.

The business solutions were pretty straightforward: farmers and cheesemakers needed resources for equipment, product development, and, in most cases, support and encouragement.

Another element in helping the cheese business thrive is the incubator, like the one run by Cedar Grove's Bob Wills, whom we will talk about shortly. Wills has made the most of his facility by opening it to fledgling cheesemakers, some of whom have grown into superstars like Willi Lehner of Bleu Mont and Mike Gingrich of Uplands Cheese Company.

Wow Your Guests with an Artisan Cheese Course

Jeanne Carpenter is a woman after my own heart. We share the fundamental belief that the best food comes with a story. Not anonymous food that comes from a factory far, far away, but food that comes from a person with a quirky personality and interesting story to tell. That, she says, makes the best cheese course.

The story behind your own cheese might be as simple as the tasting at the cheese shop where you learned from the cheesemonger, or how you found the cheese at a farmers' market. Of course, visiting the cheesemaking facility or the farm makes the best story. Cheese Underground, Carpenter's popular blog, is a great source for ideas.

And whereas the traditional cheese plate may have a trio of creamy soft, nutty hard, and bold blue, Carpenter suggests switching it up to focus on the milk and serve a cow, sheep, and goat mix. Furthermore, if you have access to a great cheesemonger who showcases midwestern cheese, you could go beyond Wisconsin to enjoy cheeses from other states. Try a goat quartet of Capriole's Wabash Cannonball from Indiana, Prairie Fruit Farm's Little Bloom on the Prairie from Illinois, Reichert's Dairy Aire from Iowa, and Fantome's fresh goat cheese from Wisconsin. Taste the cheese in order of mildest to strongest flavor for the full effect.

Perhaps the most prominent farmers' market "graduate" is Mike Gingrich, award-winning master cheesemaker from **Uplands Cheese Company**. He created Pleasant Ridge Reserve, a farmstead cheese made only from the milk of pasture-grazed cows on his farm. This Beaufort-style cheese has won best in show in the American Cheese Society competition an astounding three times. To put the achievement in perspective, no other cheese has won more than once. Gingrich, along with his wife, Carol, and their herd-managing partners, Dan and Jeanne Patenaude, used to drive four hours each way to Chicago's Green City Market to sell their then-new cheese. As with many budding food entrepreneurs, the folks at Uplands used farmers'

Pleasant Ridge Reserve at Uplands Cheese Company

markets to dip a toe into the water as they increased their capacity, at the same time developing an audience for their foods.

Gingrich came from a farming background but spent some successful years with Xerox. When most people kick back and relax, Gingrich studied to be Wisconsin's first certified cheesemaker, and ten years after launching the Uplands Cheese Company, he has not looked back.

When I first met Gingrich and his cheese at the Green City Market's winter market, his Pleasant Ridge Reserve was $14 a pound. Today it is about twice that much, and worth every penny.

Gingrich must have had an eye on succession strategy when he brought in Andy Hatch, a talented cheesemaker. Hatch's Rush Creek Reserve, modeled after the French cheese Vacheron Mont d'Or, is aged-wrapped in spruce bark; another seasonal cheese, it debuted in late fall 2010. Hatch recommends it with a Riesling, Gewürztraminer, or malty beer.

Cheesemaker rock star Mike Gingrich of Uplands Cheese Company

Mineral Point Farmers' Market

Since 1996

15 vendors

Saturdays, May through October

Water Tower Park, Highway 151 at Madison Street

One of the fixtures at this market is Rink DaVee of **Shooting Star Farm** in Mineral Point, Wisconsin, a farmer with movie-star looks and downtown business savvy. An acolyte of Alice Waters who scouted and farmed for Chez Panisse, DaVee is a founder of Homegrown Wisconsin, a cooperative of more than thirty organic growers surrounding Madison. He used his experience with this business model as a springboard into the private business venture Green & Green, where he sources foods from Madison-area farms and creameries and then delivers them to Chicago-area restaurants. Speaking of green, DaVee is known for spectacular salad greens.

The market also features **King's Hill Farm**, **Driftless Ridge Farm**, and **Bures Berry Patch**, Black Angus beef from **Marr's Valley View Farms**, as well as artisans and other food vendors.

Platteville Farmers' Market

South and west of Mineral Point, we find the Platteville Farmers' Market in a public square established about 160 years ago. Relax on a park bench and plot your shopping strategy over a pastry from **Hickory Acres Farms** or a whoopie pie from **Pleasant Valley Greenhouse**. **Safe Home Farm** grows dozens of vegetables from asparagus to zucchini, as well as herbs, berries, and native plants. **Gary Olson** has sold at the Platteville market since 1980, featuring foods from his two-acre garden, orchard, and beehives. **The Driftless Market** also operates a small grocery store and deli in downtown Platteville, showcasing local foods. **Jim Stecklein** brings in free-range eggs; **Mary Schmidtke** and **Nancy Collingbourne** offer beef from Scottish Highland cattle. In the spring be sure to purchase some morel mushrooms foraged by **Roger Lange**. The market features gallery-quality art the first Saturday of each month.

35+ vendors

Saturdays, May through October

Platteville's City Park in front of the Platteville Municipal Building

Viroqua Farmers' Market

For garlic fans, your highlight will be more than fifty varieties of garlic from **Randall Olson**. **Two Brothers Orchard** sells organic cherries, raspberries, and apples. **Valley of Joy Farm** sells natural honey and beeswax candles, plus kale, turnips, and broad beans. You will also find Amish-made furniture.

50+ vendors

Saturdays, June through October

220 Main Street, Viroqua

Organic Valley, La Farge

Kelly Gibson shops at the Viroqua Farmers' Market, as do a lot of staffers at Organic Valley, the nation's largest cooperative of organic dairy farmers. Gibson's position is perfect for her background as cofounder of the Slow Food Chicago chapter and longtime national board member. She says she has more than sixteen hundred bosses, referring to the dairy farm members of Organic Valley and Organic Prairie, its meat-producing group.

Kelly Gibson, staffer at Organic Valley Family of Farms

Gibson's role is to nurture relationships with like-minded organizations such as the Rodale Institute, founded by organic pioneer J. I. Rodale, who also began the publishing empire that includes Prevention and Organic Gardening magazines, as well as the Environmental Working Group, a team of scientists and policy experts who use public information to identify facts of importance to the environment. All her responsibilities aim to forward sustainable, organic agriculture.

Organic Valley also reaches out to its local community and other organic fans by hosting an annual country fair on its grounds. The Kickapoo Country Fair is an annual thank-you party for the region's residents and a celebration of local organic food. The nearby Kickapoo River gives the country fair its name. The river, in turn, is named for the native American Indian tribe of the region, meaning "one that comes and goes," perfect for the meandering river and for the tribe.

George Siemon founded Organic Valley in 1988 with a simple premise: keep family farmers farming, and advocate for humane animal treatment and environmental stewardship. He started by banding together a handful of farmers in southwest Wisconsin and now leads a national cooperative and has expanded into meat products under the banner Organic Prairie.

A sea of sunflowers in a neighboring field will be used for fuel at Organic Valley's headquarters, a green building that fits well into the Wisconsin landscape.

At Organic Valley's headquarters in LaFarge

Eau Claire Downtown Farmers' Market

70+ vendors

Wednesdays, Thursdays, and Saturdays, June through October (plus Saturdays in May)

300 Riverfront Terrace in Phoenix Park, Eau Claire

The covered, skylighted pavilion of the Eau Claire downtown markets shelters about seventy vendors, including **Bullfrog Fish Farm**, which produces rainbow trout in the cool waters of the Chippewa Valley. **Sylvan Hills Organic Vegetables** has been growing a range of vegetables in clay loam since 2000. **Hillview Farm** sells apples and apple products, including cider, as well rhubarb, plums, and sour cherries. **Castle Rock Organic Dairy** sells milk and cheese (certified organic by MOSA, the Midwest Organic Services Association) and offers home delivery to patrons in the Eau Claire area. Third-generation farmers Mark and Andrea Nyseth own **Blueberry Ridge Orchard** and offer six varieties of blueberries: Patriot, Northland, Blueray, Toro, Bluecrop, and Nelson. Be sure to score a creamy treat from **9 Degrees**, a local version of the ice cream cart, showcasing hand-dipped cones of ice cream made from **Timm's Dairy** milk.

Downtown Appleton Farm Market

90+ vendors

Saturdays, June through October; indoors at City Center November through March

College Avenue from Appleton Street to Durkee Street, Appleton

Food adventurers will find elk burgers, sausages, steaks, and roasts from **Navarino Valley Elk Ranch** and fresh trout from **Wilderness Springs**. Snap up vegetables from a number of vendors, including **Pang and Lee Kue**, **Yia Vang**, and **Chang's Produce**. Find meat and cheese at **Venneford Farms**.

Delafield Farmers' Market

The Delafield Market requires vendors to be from fewer than fifty miles away. At the beginning of the season, get your garden going with **Judy's Blooms.** In the fall, look for **BB Caramels** by Bretta Watterson, the perfect complement to any of fourteen varieties of apples from **Sha-Ray Orchard**, which has been family owned since 1952. Honey is available year round from **Eickstedt's Honey Knoll Farm**, **BrynTeg Farm**, and **Aunt Bee's Honey**, which also offers honey lotion and lip balm. If shopping makes you hungry, choose from **Song's Kettle Corn**, **Kathryn's** egg rolls and spring rolls, or John Zamorski's **ZBQ** smoked pork and brisket. You will also find handmade soap, candles, wood furniture, and birdhouses. Live music contributes to the festive setting in this historic downtown.

Founded 1991

20+ farm vendors, plus artisans

Saturdays, May through October

Main and Dopkins Streets, Delafield

The Urban Farming Genius of Milwaukee

Growing Power Farm Market

5500 W. Silver Spring Drive

Founded 1999

Growing Power in Milwaukee is housed on the last remaining farm within Milwaukee's city limits, and the two-acre parcel is directly in the middle of an urban neighborhood. It is here that Will Allen makes his magic.

Will Allen, urban farming evangelist

To call Will Allen an urban farmer would be wrong. Well, it would be technically correct, because he is the nation's most famous urban farmer, but *evangelist* would be a much better term for someone who is so infectious with enthusiasm.

Allen bought the farm that has become Growing Power headquarters as a place to sell some of his vegetables he grew on one hundred acres farther out of town. In 1993 this place would have been considered a food desert: there was no nearby grocery store selling fresh food. "I thought it would be a good place to sell vegetables and maybe hire some of the neighbor kids," says Allen.

When I asked about how he got the idea for Growing Power, with its massive composting program, plans for a five-story vertical farm, and $12 million capital development campaign, I expected a story of some epiphany that stemmed from his early years as the sixth son of South Carolina sharecroppers, or perhaps a vision of how to parlay the business savvy he honed during his years at Procter & Gamble into a farming empire.

The answer was much simpler: "It just evolved," he says. "I bought the last remaining farm in Milwaukee. I was only the third owner. I sold bedding plants and vegetables and connected with a youth group." After that YWCA youth group came a partnership with Heifer International to produce worms and fish. One thing led to another, and then came the grants—first, one from the Ford Foundation, then the genius grant from the MacArthur Foundation, and after that one from the Kellogg Foundation. After that? An invitation to the White House, of course. First Lady Michelle Obama invited him to participate in her efforts to remake our country's food system.

Time 100, the magazine's list that has included U.S. presidents, Nobel laureates, and CEOs of powerful tech companies, listed Allen along with South Africa's Nelson Mandela and Buddhist leader the Dalai Lama, who was also born to farming parents—esteemed company indeed.

Despite all his grandiose plans, though, Allen's first recommendation is that people who want to eat good food should grow some. "Especially if you want your children to stay healthy, you should introduce healthy food early," says Allen. "Young people especially get it. Today, 60 percent of the good food revolution is under age forty. Ten years ago, it was all academics and farmers."

Step into Growing Power's Milwaukee headquarters and you would be surprised at the abundance behind such a humble façade in a neighborhood some describe as gritty. Hydroponics, vermiculture, and composting all have designated zones, and tilapia swim in a twelve-foot-diameter swimming pool, line caught to order by the CEO himself. Greenhouses shelter twelve thousand pots of herbs and salad mix. Goats, rabbits, and turkeys are raised for food.

Growing Power sells at two farmers' markets in Milwaukee and four in Chicago and operates a popular market-basket program. And now Allen's organization also operates farms at a boys' and girls' camp, school, and community gardens, and an "art on the farm" *potager* in Grant Park. Erika Allen, Will's daughter, runs the Chicago programs, which include the Grant Park garden as well as one near the Cabrini Green neighborhood on a former basketball court. The above-ground garden features worm-system raised beds using Growing Power's soil from composted food waste and coffee grounds from restaurants, and leftover barley from Milwaukee breweries.

What Is Next?

What is next for America's farmers' markets? The path was laid for
the current explosion in 1976 by an act of Congress, which makes
sense, given the back-to-the-land movement of the time, the eleva-
tion of food prices, and the disillusionment from the Vietnam War and
Watergate.

The farmers' market phenomenon is fed by a classic duality of
carrot-or-stick motivations. The carrot in this analogy is the allure of
fresh, luscious, well-grown food, the relationship with local producers,
and the feeling of participating in a healthful community and having
relationships with people who live with their hands in the soil. The
stick part is the alarming side of industrialized food production, the
growing incidence of foodborne illness, the concerns about animal
welfare, and the environmental impact of confinement operations, all
of which feed into a need to have more control over how our food is
produced. The more consumers learn, the more they vote with their
wallets to live in alliance with their values, whether those values
embrace flavor or ethics, or something else. And thus we have the
boom we see today.

The broader economics are changing, too. American Farmland Trust's Julia Freedgood adds another perspective. "Thirty or forty years ago, vegetable processors probably made the economic decision to concentrate growing in California's Central Valley because of its year-round season," she says. "Now with shipping costs and demands for local food, that trend is reversing."

Another challenge, says Rich Pirog of the Leopold Center in Iowa, is to reduce the fear in the banking industry by communicating business plans that show a strong potential for profit. "There's not much data yet, and so bankers are leery of financing agriculture ventures," he says. While working toward that goal, many small-scale initiatives are funded by grants, and recipients need to demonstrate how they will carry on once the grant funding runs out, he adds.

Jim Slama, a longtime advocate of small farms, added a financing element to the Financing Farm to Fork seminar as part of the annual Family Farmed Expo held in Chicago each spring. The 2010 seminar illustrated that the local food movement has reached a tipping point, with standing room only at the keynote address by Kathleen Merrigan, Deputy Secretary of Agriculture, known for her support of small farmers. Under her guidance, the USDA's Know Your Farmer, Know Your Food program has taken shape to showcase the smaller side of agriculture. Merrigan reiterated that there is work to be done.

Building Better Business Models

Once our communities are saturated with farmers' markets, chances are they will still only represent about 3 percent of our food sales. For local food to be the norm again, as it was generations ago, more people need to buy from growers. But what about people who cannot get to a farmers' market, like my TV-cameraman brother who works crazy hours, or the woman in my cooking class who had three kids in sports on Saturday morning?

In some cases it is a virtual food hub, where people order and pay online, then pick up their order as they would a CSA share. Some food hubs even deliver. In the Midwest, food hubs like **Harvest Michigan**, **Irv & Shelly's Fresh Picks** in Chicago, **Local D'Lish** in Minneapolis, and **Farm to Family Naturally** in St. Louis, all focus on finding new ways to get local food into eager stomachs. Computer software is becoming more sophisticated to help hubs increase their ordering capabilities.

Farm-to-Office Eating: FarmShare Ohio

Some solutions are as simple as bringing a farmers' market experience to those who do not have a market near them. Kari Moore started her **FarmShare Ohio** business in Cleveland to deliver bags of farmers' market food to workers in the Tower City office complex in the heart of downtown Cleveland. People can subscribe to a weekly bag, or stop by from week to week.

Kari Moore shares her own story:

> I have worked with local farmers and food producers since 2002, helping connect them with local market opportunities throughout the region. Over the years, I met a lot of farmers who were growing beautiful food that didn't always find a good home. Maybe they were rained out at their weekly farmers' market, maybe they just weren't connected with the right customers, or perhaps they planted a few too many tomatoes and just couldn't move them all quickly enough.
>
> About the same time, I was also meeting many folks who really wanted to eat locally and seasonally, but just didn't have a practical way to do so. People are busy. But folks still want local blueberries. And not everyone has the time to corral the kids and get to the farmers' market each Saturday morning by 10 a.m. before the blueberries sell out.
>
> I founded FarmShare with the intent of making local eating more convenient by bringing farm-fresh, locally grown food to convenient locations. We started out at Tower City as a way to reach the downtown business community. There's nothing better than having a beautiful bag of fresh, local produce and artisan bread waiting for you on your way home from work. This year, we're going a bit hyper-local with the FarmShare concept, offering an east-side pickup location at Fire that's convenient for our neighbors in Cleveland Heights. And because we have family in Independence, we decided to offer a FarmShare pickup there as well. From the beginning, I've really just wanted my family, friends, and neighbors to have as much fun as I do eating locally and seasonally.
>
> Through FarmShare I also try provide a bit of predictability in a very unpredictable business called farming. We encourage our FarmShare subscribers to commit for the season, and that way, we can place a standing order with our farms for a set amount of produce each week. Our farmers then know how much to plant, and they can count on FarmShare to be here for them each week, for the duration of the season.

Minestra alla Toscana

Stefano Vigletti, Trattoria Stefano, Il Ritrovo, and Field to Fork, Sheboygan.

One of Simply Wisconsin's restaurant patrons is Stefano Vigletti, who has an impressive four-restaurant empire in charming Sheboygan, on the western shore of Lake Michigan about half way between Milwaukee and Green Bay.

Beans/brodo

¾ pound dried cannellini beans

4 sage leaves

2 cloves garlic

Sea salt to taste

2 tablespoons extra virgin olive oil

Base

¼ cup extra virgin olive oil

2 large carrots, diced into ¼-inch pieces (approx. 2 cups)

2 ribs celery, finely chopped (1½–2 cups)

2 medium onions, finely chopped (2 cups)

1 clove garlic, sliced

¼ cup Italian parsley, finely chopped

1½ teaspoons fresh sage, chopped

Soup

1 cup diced Yukon gold potatoes (½-inch pieces)

2 cups chopped Savoy cabbage

1 cup green beans, chopped into bite-sized pieces

1½ cups zucchini, diced into ½-inch pieces

1½ cups gold zucchini, diced into ½-inch pieces, or yellow summer squash

1 28-oz. can San Marzano tomatoes, chopped with juice reserved

3 cups chopped Tuscan kale, such as Lacinato, or Swiss chard

This robust vegetable stew is perfect for simmering on an autumn afternoon. It is best served the second day, when all the flavors have melded, so plan accordingly. Chef Vigletti buys his ingredients from Springdale Farms in Plymouth as well as Simply Wisconsin.

To prepare the beans, soak them overnight in cold water. Drain and rinse. Cover with four inches of cold water. Add olive oil, sage, garlic and salt. Bring to a boil, then reduce heat and simmer until beans are fork tender, about 1-1½ hours, skimming off any foam that appears. Puree one quarter of the beans with a bit of the bean liquid. Set aside puree and the beans in bean water.

To make the base, use your largest soup pot over medium heat. Preheat pan and add olive oil, and then sauté the carrots, celery, onion, and garlic with the parsley and sage until very tender, about 20-25 minutes, seasoning to taste.

To "assemble" the soup, season with a bit of salt and pepper after adding each of the ingredients. Add potatoes and sauté 4-5 minutes. Add cabbage and green beans and cook covered for 5-7 minutes. Add zucchini and/or squash and sauté uncovered for 5 minutes. Add tomatoes and juice, simmering until saucy and reduced slightly, about 3-4 minutes. Add kale and a bit of bean water if necessary to moisten ingredients and to prevent sticking, but *do not stir.* Cover, allowing kale to cook for 5-7 minutes. Now stir together, adding bean puree. Using a slotted spoon, scoop in all the cooked beans, and add enough bean water to achieve a rather thick stew. Adjust salt and pepper to taste and simmer for 20-25 minutes. Ladle into bowls and drizzle with extra virgin olive oil.

A Truck and a Dream: Homegrown Wisconsin

In some cases, the solution is for the farmers to band together, as they have with cooperatives for generations. In the mid-1990s, about thirteen farmers in the area surrounding Madison had maximized what they could sell to their restaurant patrons, but they still had food to sell. They pooled their resources and hired a truck and driver to take fruits and vegetables to the Chicago area, thus boosting their income without having thirteen farmers make the trek every week.

In terms of a carbon footprint, this is good news, but it also offered the small farmers the benefit of sharing resources. Chicago is a six-hour round trip, and many farmers could not be away from their farms an entire day each week, particularly if they also worked farmers' markets. And chefs loved Homegrown Wisconsin's streamlined ordering system and consolidated delivery. "We wished all farms could be as organized," they said.

The group grew to more than thirty farms selling to sixteen restaurants in the Chicago area. Later they transitioned to a CSA operation, and in 2009 Deb Hanson bought the operation and now sells to about thirty restaurants from Milwaukee to Madison and Chicago under the banner Simply Wisconsin.

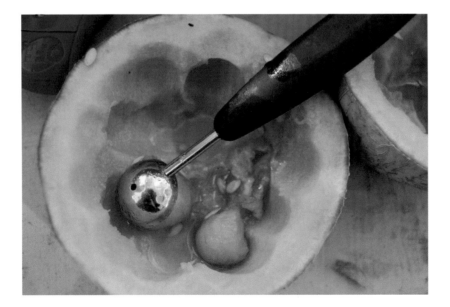

Starting with the Next Generation

Bringing local food to schools has been the goal of parents and educators for decades. Alice Waters founded the Edible Schoolyard in Berkeley, California in 1995 to serve Martin Luther King Jr. Middle School. The one-acre garden is often held up as the epitome of school gardens, but Alice Waters once told me that the annual budget for this garden is $100,000. In this case funding comes from Waters's Chez Panisse Foundation and is leveraged by her star power in the food world and a ten-person staff. But the mere thought is staggering for any teacher who wants to educate students about how to produce food. And of course there is also the challenge of who weeds and waters when school is out of session. That said, school gardens seem to have caught on as a teaching tool.

One Michigander took a connection to food a step further. After leaving Grand Rapids, Michigan, for graduate school in England, Sara Elizabeth Ippel became enthralled with the international camaraderie there. She then set out to visit eighty countries and came back to the states to settle in Chicago and make her mark. Three years and three proposals later, she established the **Academy for Global Citizenship** as a charter school on Chicago's southwest side.

The school operates a longer school year and a longer day schedule to make time for classes centered on environmental stewardship, such as rooftop chickens on the green roof, a schoolyard garden, and organic breakfasts and lunches. Cafeteria cooks work with local farmers, who see the wisdom in making a good price for additional food for weekly subscription boxes for the families. Parents can take cooking classes the school offers with an eye on nourishing healthy bodies to support growing minds. In an area where more than 80 percent of students qualify for free or reduced school lunches, this is quite an accomplishment.

A Business Based on One Long Table

With all the focus on distribution channels, and education, sometimes the way to entice people is through taste. Local food boosterism needs cheerleaders showcasing artisan foods, to simply delight the senses. Slow Food takes this approach.

Portia Belloc Lowndes has built a business based on one long table, the Slow Food philosophy of sitting down together over good food and conversation. She founded **Pitchfork Productions** by taking a page from her years as co-leader of Slow Food Chicago to host family style dinners at farms in Wisconsin, Illinois, Indiana, and Michigan prepared by chefs who have worked with the host farm.

Because it's the sitting together and enjoying the taste of the earth, preserving a connection to our growers and each other, that make it worth the effort.

Index